In loving memory of my mom

I love you.

Table of Contents

- Introduction 12
- Thus, It Begins 12
- Step by Step 13
- My Experience with Midlife 15
- Resolved to Stand 16
- Divine Intervention 17
- A Pioneer in the Movement 18
- Never Alone 20
- Chapter 1 21
- Growth Scripts 21
- From Past to Present 23
- The Path to Maturity 24
- The Years of Midlife | Course Adjustment 25
- The Years of Midlife | Crisis 26
- The Beginning of the Crisis for the Midlife Spouse 28
- The Beginning of the Crisis for the Left-behind Spouse 29
- How to use this Book 31
- Encouragement 32
- Chapter 2 33
- Recognizing Growth Scripts 33
- The Hallmarks of the Crisis 34
- The Emotional Development Process 35

Explanation of the Stages of the Midlife Crisis 36
The Stages of a Midlife Crisis 37
Roadmaps and Timelines 37
The Role of the Left-behind Spouse 39
Encouragement 40
Chapter 3 41
Stages of a Mid-Life Crisis 41
Stage 1 | A Change of Perception 41
Stage 2 | Loss of Emotional Control 44
Stage 3 | Total Emotional Regression 46
First Emotional Awakening 50
Stage 4 | Facing Total Failure 51
Stage 5 | Introspection 53
The Process of Creating Space for Change, Growth and Becoming 57
Stage 6 | The Final Facing 57
Phase 1: The Final Disintegration 58
The Second Emotional Awakening 59
Phase 2: The Final Temptations 59
Process of Re-bonding 62
Exiting the Midlife Storm 62
Phase 3: The Final Fears 63
Chapter 4 66
Stage 7 | The Settling Down Process 66

Post Crisis: The Couple Aspect 68

Stage 8 | The Final Inner Healing 70

One Midlife Crisis, Different Possibilities 74

Chapter 5 78

Who are these "Children" 78

The Child versus the Core Personality 80

THE PROCESS OF RESOLUTION DURING THE CRISIS 81

The Past Issues of the Midlife Spouse 81

The Children of their Issues 82

Emotional History Repeats 84

Emotional Scattering and Regathering 85

The Appearance and Behavior of the Children 86

Resolving the Children 88

Recognizing the Children 89

Wisdom for the Left-behind Spouse 90

Chapter 6 93

The Peak of the Midlife Crisis 93

Left-behind Spouse Forced into their own Journey 95

Midlife Crisis | Crossroads 96

Dead End Roads 98

The First Awakening | Awakening to Self 99

Observations of the Left-behind Spouse 101

Chapter 7 104

Controlling Behaviors of the Midlife Crisis 104
Anger and Spewing 105
Blame Shifting 108
Chaos 108
Confusion 109
Control and Manipulation 110
Defensiveness 112
Deflection 113
Double Standard 113
Drama 115
Response of the Left-behind Spouse to Controlling Behaviors 118
Encouragement 120
Chapter 8 121
Abandonment 122
Response of the Left-behind Spouse to Abandonment 123
Alcohol and Drugs 124
Emotional Splitting 125
Response of the Left-behind Spouse to Emotional Splitting 126
Escape and Avoid Tactics 126
Response of the Left-behind Spouse to Escape and Avoid Tactics 127
Opposite Behaviors 127
Response of the Left-behind Spouse to Opposite Behaviors 129
Spending 130

Response of the Left-behind Spouse to Spending 130

Vanishing 131

Response of the Left-behind Spouse to Vanishing 132

Wearing the Mask 132

Public Versus Private Mask 133

Response of the Left-behind Spouse to Wearing the Mask 134

Chapter 9 135

Teen vs. Midlife Similarities 135

Response of Left-behind Spouse to Behavioral Cycling 136

Piecing Things Together 138

Puzzle Piece Analogy 140

The Need for Space 142

The Purpose of Cycling | Emotional Rebuilding of Self 144

From Repression to Resolution 145

Chapter 10 147

Emotional Imbalance 148

The Search for Outside Solutions 149

The Children of their Issues | Affair 150

Core Character Compromised 151

Brief Overview of the Midlife Affair 153

Cake-Eating 154

The Marriage Breakdown 155

Response of Left-behind Spouse to the Midlife Affair 156

Chapter 11 158
Choice of the Midlife Spouse to Stay or Leave 158
The Stages of an Affair 159
Timeline for the Affair 161
The Affair Partner 163
Infatuation is not Unconditional Love 164
The Foundation of the Affair 166
Masks and Mirroring Behavior 167
The Affair Addiction 168
More Responses of Left-behind Spouse to the Midlife Affair 169
The Affair Breakdown 171
Breaking the Affair Addiction 173
The Strange Connection 176
After Effects of the Affair 177
Chapter 12 178
The Venture into Sin 179
The Trek into Adultery 180
The Dead End of Adultery 182
The Consequences of Adultery 183
Consequences for The Affair Partner 184
Response for the Left-behind Spouse to the Consequences 185
Chapter 13 186
The Turn Toward Home 186

The Return Home	188
The Harder Work	189
Walking the Emotional Tightrope	191
Slow Moves Forward	192
Reconciliation | It Takes Two	194
Positives for the Midlife Spouse	196
Positives for the Left-behind Spouse	196
Hearts Blessing | An Unwanted Journey	198
The Call to Change from the Inside Out	200
The Internal Mirror of Reflection	201
The Emotional Road of Hell	202
Walking This Journey in Grace and Understanding	203
Dedication	204
Chapter 14	205
Thus, It Begins with You	205
The Journey to Wholeness and Healing	207
The Way Forward	207
The Journey of Both Spouses are Attached	208
Becoming the Opposite	210
Questions to Consider in the Journey Forward	211
Chapter 15	212
Marriage and God | The Marital Covenant	214
It Takes Two | The Marital Covenant	215

Called to Stand | The Marital Covenant	216
To Stand or Not to Stand	218
The Determined Stanchion	218
Why Divorce does not have to end a Stand	220
Midlife Spouse Remarriage to Affair Partner	224
Left-behind Spouse Remarriage to Another	227
Chapter 16	228
Eight Stages of Healing for the Left-behind Spouse	228
Stage 1. Full Emotional Devastation	229
The Emotional Bomb	229
Their Script | Your Pain	230
Steps for Moving Forward	234
Stage 2. Denial	234
Stage 3. Bargaining	235
Stage 4. Emotional Rock Bottom	236
Stage 5. In Deep Mourning	237
Stage 6. Crossroad of Choice	237
Stage 7. Begin Journey toward Wholeness and Healing	239
Emotions Triggered Within these Stages	239
Reality of Past Self	240
Change, Growth and Becoming	242
Steps Toward Healing	242
Steps Toward Healing	244

Reality of past Marital Dynamics 244
Steps Toward Healing 246
The Crossroad of Decision... 246
Am I Still Willing to Stand for this Marriage?... 247
Moving into the Second Half of the Journey 248
Encouragement.. 248
Stage 8. Acceptance, Forgiveness and Healing... 249
Acceptance... 249
Forgiveness 249
Healing 251
Emotional Triggers 252
The Healing Process 253
Steps to Process and Heal from Emotional Triggers................................ 253
Detachment 254
Why and How to Detach 256
Why Detach?.. 257
Communication in Detachment... 258
No Contact 258
No Initiating Contact... 260
Go Dim 260
Go Dark 260
Emotional Repackaging | Living Authentically... 261
Reclaim Personal Identity 262

Reclaiming Emotional Power 263
Reclaiming and Defending Self-Respect 263
Godly Intuition 265
Final Emotional Processing 266
Chapter 17 268
Boundaries 270
Boundaries Covered in this Chapter 272
Boundaries: Behavioral and Relational 273
Boundaries: Behavioral Cycling 274
Boundaries: Children of their Issues 275
Boundaries: Disrespect 276
Boundaries: Guard Your Heart 276
Boundaries: Midlife Affair 277
Boundaries: Revolving Door 278
Boundaries: Separation of "Me and Thee" 279
Boundaries: Self-Care 280
Life's Lesson: Change 281
Life's Lesson: Control 283
Life's Lesson: Letting Go 284
Life's Lesson: Unconditional Love for God, Self and Others 285

Introduction

There is hope as long as there is love within your heart.

Thus, It Begins

This book is written to help people learn about the midlife crisis and find support navigating through. It covers the stages, aspects, and lessons of the crisis and explains how and why the crisis begins and ends.[1] Through reading, one will gain a deeper understanding of the midlife crisis, find answers, and learn to cope with the various antics and behaviors of their spouse. These antics include, but are not limited to, anger, projection, regressive behaviors, midlife affair, and more.

If your spouse is between the age of 35 and 55 and acting out of the ordinary, or if you've been subjected to the "emotional bomb"[2] that has devastated you ("I love you but I'm not in love with you" or something similar), your spouse is most likely going through a midlife crisis.[3] (If you are uncertain this is your situation, there are signs and indicators, also called Hallmarks, to help you determine if this is indeed what you are facing. Turn to the chapter entitled "The Hallmarks of the Crisis" to learn more.)

---

[1] Not all midlife crisis situations resolve in a successful ending. More on this in chapters to come.
[2] Emotional bomb – phrases such as, "I love you but I'm not in love with you."
[3] Midlife crisis is not a medically recognized term, nor can it be "fixed" by anyone except the person going directly this crisis.

This book is written specifically for you, the left-behind spouse of someone in midlife crisis. This is a book of knowledge and understanding, broken down by the one going through the midlife crisis and the left-behind spouse (you). Your midlife spouse will not be open to learning or understanding their crisis, they will deny they are in crisis, and that's okay. Their crisis is all about them and it is their journey to take, in God's way and in God's time. Just as your journey, which began with the "emotional bomb", is all about you. Hold on to what you learn, apply the teachings within, and focus on your own journey to wholeness and healing.[1]

Step by Step

Your mind will work overtime to figure out what happened, the behavior of your spouse, and what you could have done differently to save the marriage. You will read many things you do not want to accept as truth. You may throw the book against the wall, only to later retrieve it and try again to read, learn and understand. This is normal behavior, as it is difficult to understand and accept your spouse's damaging behaviors that are beyond your control.

You will return to these pages many times during this season, each time to discover the explanations make more sense and resonate more with your journey. The temptation will be to read through this book and pick out where your midlife spouse is in their journey, trying to push them forward. **A word of caution:** If your spouse in crisis is not at that stage, the push will not birth results and you will

---

[1] The journey to wholeness and healing is covered in more depth in subsequent chapters.

be reminded, once again, that everything falls into place only when it is supposed to – not any earlier than its set time.

The more you understand the midlife process, the better equipped you are to survive and grow through the pain of this raw journey. Many emotions within you, including fear, will be exposed. You will come to understand this is also your season of growth. You will feel pressure to grow, change and become all you were created to be as you move your focus from your midlife spouse to yourself. You will begin looking to make lasting changes to push you into the last half of your life. Hold tightly to the Lord and take this journey step by step, day by day.

This road is long and hard. The obstacles seem insurmountable, and the crisis will seem to last forever. Don't rush through this journey, as pushing yourself and your midlife spouse will cause steps to wholeness and healing to be missed, and the journey will be prolonged.

This book will enlighten you, but the Lord is your best Guide to carry you through this, the toughest battle of your life. At the end of this journey, your old wounds will be healed, and you will be changed for the better, emotionally and spiritually.

There is hope as long as you love your midlife spouse and are willing to learn the life's lessons set before you as a result of your spouse's crisis.

My Experience with Midlife

In 1999, my husband faced a major life's event which triggered a three-year midlife crisis. At the time, I was hardheaded and stubborn, thinking I knew it all. The more I rebelled, the worse the situation became. The midlife crisis was difficult for me to understand. There wasn't much written on the subject, and it wasn't spoken of. People knew it happened, but most didn't know why it happened. People with information about it were in short supply and information on the internet was limited. The only information within mainstream media on this topic was a book written by Jim Conway entitled, "Men in Midlife Crisis."[1] I found a few other articles, but the writing and explanations were not clear.

In His mercy, the Lord sent me a spiritual guide who helped me reach a place of understanding. It was as if she knew me better than I knew myself and didn't expect me to grasp all the advice at one time. She knew that, in this situation, it takes time to pull it all together. Eventually, I surrendered the situation to God, and He taught me to navigate through the journey of a lifetime.

In 2002, my husband exited his midlife crisis. But he came out of the crisis with one unresolved issue and, in less than two years, that issue returned to torment him.[2] I was in my own midlife transition when my husband headed back into his second midlife crisis. This second time was worse than before, and our marriage hit a low

---

[1] Conway, Jim. Midlife Crisis in Men. Cook Communications, 1985.
[2] This will make more sense as you gain understanding.

point. I was at a crossroads in deciding whether to leave or stay in the marriage.

Resolved to Stand

An important part of honoring one's marriage vows is to look for ways to pull the marriage out of the fire rather than seeking excuses to leave it. I made the decision to stand on the foundation of marriage.

When I made it clear that I was making a stand in hopes of a restored marriage, I was met with disbelief, name-calling and second-guessing from acquaintances. Over and over, I answered the question, "Why do you want to stay in a marriage that is not working?" When I explained that I was obeying my Godly intuition,[1] I was met with laughter and ridicule of hearing voices that were not present. My faith and belief in God came under attack. I was told I needed to "exercise caution when trusting the Lord with my marital situation."

Because I refused to walk out, throw him out, or end my marriage in divorce, I was often accused of being stuck. When I insisted God would bring me through the trial with a restored marriage, I was told I was addicted to emotional pain. The longer I stood for the marriage, the more hate I endured. None of these things were true. I was learning the lessons of a lifetime[2] within the vehicle of standing for my marriage.

---

[1] Godly intuition will be further explained in later chapters.
[2] The lessons of a lifetime are covered in more depth in subsequent chapters.

Divine Intervention

God intervened in multiple ways. He did not intend for the solution to come through divorce. He showed me an outcome of marital restoration if I would walk the hard road forward and obey Him in all things. He continually encouraged, *"There is hope as long as there is love within your heart."*

God could not have worked in my situation had I not agreed to stand aside and give Him control. After three months of fighting against His will, I surrendered to walking my own journey toward wholeness and healing. This journey taught me to focus on myself rather than my midlife spouse. God was my counselor who taught me how to access my inner Self and find the hidden and buried issues from my childhood. He showed me how changes made on the inside would resolve my outside issues. And He told me the changes made were for me, not anyone else.

I learned to detach, distance, let go, and let God work on my husband. I learned to separate my husband's midlife behaviors from the person he truly was. I learned to set boundaries on the behaviors that directly affected me, while releasing the rest. *The world teaches us to hold on with all our might; the Bible teaches us to let go.* I had to release my midlife spouse to God so work could be done within both of us, separately and individually, yet at the same time.

My husband and I spent twelve years in the midlife grind, traveling a long road that was hard on both of us. The Lord restored our marriage completely. We are still together, fully reconciled, and our marriage is thriving. We have been together for over 30 years. It has been well worth the journey, and I have no regrets for standing as long as it took to attain the better marriage I was hopeful for.

People wonder if a marriage can come through the midlife crisis, whole, healed and intact. My answer – yes, it can. God did not intend for all people to end their marriages during the midlife crisis. He means for as many as possible to learn to transcend this crisis with their marriage surviving this trial. When a couple comes through this crisis, they have a completely transformed marriage which becomes a source of peace, joy, and happiness. Why? Because both people have learned to find answers within Self and live from that better place moving forward.

A Pioneer in the Movement

I have had the privilege of being a pioneer in the movement to understand the stages and lessons of the midlife crisis. Most of my knowledge was gained through God, who gave me understanding and insight into the journey toward wholeness, coupled with my own emotional survival of life situations. The rest was learned by research, observation, coaching, and mentors who poured into me as I walked through my own midlife transition.

In 2002, I began researching and writing about the midlife crisis, sharing the information online. Those activities stopped when my husband exited his first round of the crisis. I laid low and focused on my own midlife transition until 2009. At that time, God called me to the work of research, writing, and coaching as a guide for left-behind spouses wanting to stand for their marriage. While that calling has never changed, it has evolved into a full and complete understanding of the aspects and purpose of the midlife crisis, and the changes that occur during the journey – for both the midlife spouse and the left-behind spouse.

I am not a licensed therapist or certified counselor, nor do I hold a degree in any form of psychology, sociology or even physiology. I cannot guarantee your marriage will survive, nor can I guarantee any sort of outcome. My writings are not to take the place of your own power to make personal decisions for yourself. I advise, but I cannot speak in absolute certainty about anything in your life. This is your life, and the information contained within is to help you make informed decisions for yourself.

I have been labeled a radical (or worse), but I write only about things I have personally seen and experienced. Explaining the various aspects within a midlife crisis is not going to make this time of life resolve any faster, but it will help you understand what you are seeing is real and not a figment of your imagination. My teachings are not theories, ideas or dreams; rather, they are facts based on my research, personal experience, and observations over an extended period.

Knowledge and time are both powerful tools in walking through this season. Grasp firmly to knowledge and learn to use the time wisely. In time you will grow, improve, and have a deepening understanding of what has happened and what will possibly happen in the future.

Never Alone

This is not a "new" trial, just new people going through it for the first time. No one wants to feel they are the only one holding on to a marriage that seems destroyed beyond repair. When my husband started his midlife crisis, God sent a mentor to help me understand what was happening and how to navigate the rough roads. Now He sends me to walk you through the crisis of your spouse and to provide encouragement for the days ahead.

Through the pages of this book, I come alongside to teach, encourage, and pray for you, while releasing you into the capable hands of God who knows and orchestrates all things. Remember, the Lord is always present. Once you learn to connect with Him on a deeper level, you will have a great Companion, Friend, and Father to accompany you every step of the way.

I am Hearts Blessing; I am a stander[1] and I believe in marriage. Coupled with the Lord's guidance, I am here to teach you about the midlife crisis, to encourage you in standing for your marriage, and to help you navigate through the lessons of life. Let us begin the journey toward greater wisdom, knowledge and understanding within the realm of the most difficult trial you will ever face.

May the Lord be honored and glorified through this, His work and teachings,
and may He bless you greatly in your journey to wholeness and healing.

Hearts Blessing   (((HUGS)))

---

[1] I am more of a Stanchion, a pillar of strength, called to shine the light for others by teaching, encouraging, and praying them through their own stand and growing them into the role of being a stanchion for others. More about that in another chapter.

Chapter 1

The midlife crisis is a journey to wholeness and healing for both spouses.

Growth Scripts

Every person follows a defined growth pattern, also known as a 'script.' This script identifies various aspects of maturity as they are navigated, including physical, mental, emotional, and spiritual growth. Sometimes these four growth patterns overlap, sometimes they lag behind each other. For instance, someone can be physically and mentally mature and moving forward in spiritual growth yet is emotionally immature. Emotional maturity is usually the last aspect people attain.

Why? Perhaps a child had parents with poor boundaries, thus forcing the child to deal with problems they were not emotionally equipped to handle or resolve. Being forced to deal with issues beyond their maturity, inner issues of emotional and mental damage were created within the child.

How? The parent may have made a mistake and blamed the child by saying, "Look at what you made me do!" This emotionally immature script shifted blame, projected responsibility, and gave wrong emotional power to a small child. The child mistakenly connected the wrong action done by their parent to something they had done, when in fact the child did nothing wrong to cause or trigger the hurtful deed. The emotional damage to the child came from someone outside the child's inner self.

The script is one of shifting blame and the inability to own one's actions and reactions. The emotionally immature child took the wrong action projected upon them by the parent, internalized it, and made it about themselves. The child was emotionally taught that whatever happened, whether it was in or out of their control, was their fault. We know the blame goes to the wrongdoer, but a small child does not know this. Because the child did not know how to cope, they self-protected by repressing the issue.

The small child did not know that resolution to their problem could be found on the inside of Self by working through the issue and realizing they did nothing wrong. Therefore, true to the script that each emotionally under-developed person follows, they looked to the outside of Self for a solution to their internal problem. They modeled the behavior they learned from the parent who projected blame on them. Until the child learns the major emotional lessons that they are not responsible for the wrong actions of others, they continue to internalize emotional damage and seek to find outside solutions to fix inside problems.

To explain it another way, the parent projected their wrongdoing onto the child, which wrongfully taught the child how to deal with mistakes. Until they learn the correct way to resolve this issue, the child will mimic this behavior and project their wrongful actions onto someone else to avoid taking responsibility for their actions. They learned to project from those who once projected on them.

The parent used emotional manipulation, guilt, shame, and blame to repeatedly abuse the child. Each time, the wound went deeper as the child emotionally suffered self-shame, self-blame and self-guilt. To add insult to injury, the emotionally immature parent literally demanded that the child stay quiet about the abusive actions to protect themselves. The child will carry the wound until they learn to heal Self through examination and resolution.

From Past to Present

Most adults have repressed emotional wounds and issues that stretch back to their childhood, often connecting to their parents or adults who raised them. These issues remained hidden because children are taught to see parents without fault, making it difficult to recognize early emotional damage in Self.

Throughout life, we are presented with transitional periods and opportunities to pause, review our past, resolve issues of pain or immaturity, and move forward into greater growth physically, spiritually, mentally and emotionally.[1] If one has experienced, seen and heard the scripted performance resulting from mature and immature actions, they recognize where someone is in their maturing process and are able to provide wisdom and instruction. If people choose not to work through their issues and learn the lessons of life, the issues will continue to cycle until the lessons are learned, utilized and exercised, or until the person passes away.

---

[1] Our spiritual growth is an ongoing process, and we will never fully attain spiritual maturity in this life. There's always more to learn and more growth available.

The Path to Maturity

The first transitional period into greater growth comes at the onset of puberty. At this stage, the repressed issues return, as the child is mature enough to deal with them. If the pubescent youngster has help working through the issues, they can be resolved. If not, the resurrected issues follow the same scripted action of once more being repressed, or buried, for later resolution. Full resolution to the issue is denied as avoidance tactics of repression are repeated.

The second call to maturity is at quarter life, or around 25 years old. At this age, the brain has matured and tries to turn the emotionally immature persons' attention toward emotional growth. Again, the young adult has an opportunity to examine their past, deal with any unresolved issues, learn the lessons centered around those issues, and move forward.

If the issues are left unresolved, the young adult experiences a sense of burden that increases as they continue the emotionally ingrained and immature patterns not outgrown during childhood or adolescence. Because the young adult is not equipped to handle life with maturity, things become progressively harder in every way imaginable. Why? Because they may be physically mature and mentally capable, but emotionally immature. They have not grown beyond the teenage developmental process in terms of thinking, being, and relating.

The downside of one's youth begins to roll out over the next ten years and the next stop is midlife, defined as the period between the mid-thirties and mid-fifties. This is a time to transition for later life, stretching from midlife to death. The midlife transition is intended to bring forth a balance of the four-part dimensions known as physical, mental, emotional and spiritual.

The Years of Midlife | Course Adjustment

For those who have learned, utilized and exercised all aspects of emotional growth, midlife presents an opportunity to make a few course adjustments. This means both spouses, at different times, have accomplished three things:

- Taken stock of the past
    During life's journey, one takes time to reflect on the past to see where they came from. This is part of life. This reflection is more subconscious than conscious, and it must be done to move forward. Reflection asks, "Is there anything that needs to be changed?" "Is there any growth needed to be accomplished?" Reflecting on both questions leads one into becoming what God intends.

- Viewed present life to see if on track
    Life's unmet goals are examined (physical, emotional, mental, and spiritual). If none exist, new goals are set. This means the past contributes to the present, and this past reflection leads into the present time. One looks to see how the past and present connect with the future.

- <u>Planning and moving forward</u>
    Because both spouses were emotionally mature before the midlife transition occurred, the transitioner's spouse will not be left-behind, but will understand that emotional growth is taking place and will continue. Space, time, and detachment temporarily occur so as not to increase the amount of stress the transitioning spouse experiences. Any time a person goes through a process of change, growth and becoming, there is emotional stress, even during an emotional course adjustment.

These are people who have accomplished their stages of life's growth without causing emotional upheaval in their families. They understand their emotions are about Self. Their character is strong enough to avoid temptation and to think through the consequences of their actions. These are the people who have successfully finished each stage as it came, from the onset of puberty into midlife. Their times of emotional growth were experienced as a bump in life's road because they followed life's program, learned their lessons and honored Self. They are prepared for the third age, which is later life.

Unfortunately, these people are rare.

<u>The Years of Midlife | Crisis</u>

For those who have not learned, utilized and exercised all aspects of emotional growth, midlife presents another opportunity to face and resolve their repressed issues from childhood and adolescence.

Remember, the goal of the midlife transition is emotional maturity. So, what has been neglected and remains unfinished will be subjected to a testing. In this transition, the midlife spouse is not given a choice of being drawn into this physical, mental, emotional and spiritual battle. However, to come out whole and healed, they are given every choice based in the free will God endowed within each person at birth.[1]

Everything becomes a challenge to the midlife spouse to see if they can rid themselves of the negative feelings based in the issues of their past. The midlife spouse questions what they were taught and who they are. But choosing to do a healthy self-examination is not on the agenda of many people because it involves looking within Self for the areas that need major improvements. It is painful to dig within Self, so throughout life, they seek to avoid this painful internal digging by repeating an old emotional habit – using outside solutions to fix inside problems.

Everyone goes into the process of an emotional transition. It's the rebellious actions and running behaviors designed to self-medicate, avoid, and escape the process that changes this into a crisis. Fear drives them to make drastic and terrible mistakes, and the midlife crisis sets in where the emotional aspect takes control and logical thinking is set aside.[2]

---

[1] People have choices, and it is important to allow each person the right to exercise their choices, whether right or wrong.
[2] The emotional aspect seems to suffer the most, and is the one most targeted by Satan, who tempts people based on their emotional strengths and weaknesses.

The Beginning of the Crisis for the Midlife Spouse

From the mildest of signs to the most overt acts, the various elements that bring forth the transition can be similar. Most of the time, it takes a major life-changing event[1] that causes a serious emotional crisis leading into the beginning stages of a midlife transition.

Signs of an emotional breakdown will often show, followed by emotional distance. These are triggered by feelings of inadequacy,[2] which include the perceived loss of control, and the blaming of Self for not being able to prevent these occurrences. If this event is a typical emotional crisis, then given space and time, the person will eventually return to a normal emotional balance. If not, the person's emotional breakdown and distancing gradually become worse, showing constant anger and desperation to control their personal environment.

In cases where there has not been a major life event, there is an increasing self-awareness and heightening of emotions. Combined with an increasing perception that time is running out, this results in the sense of something left undone.

Aging is a major issue during this time, because in their mind, if they are old, they will soon die. Physical changes begin around thirty-five, and physiology speaks of chemically based changes that alter hair, face, eyes, skin, and hormones. The outward appearance causes inner turmoil, because the inward changes made their way

---

[1] Major life events can include, but are not limited to, the death of a loved one, a near-death experience, loss of employment, or the graduation of a child.
[2] The midlife crisis is triggered by the issues within the person going through.

outside to physically reveal themselves. What happens on the outside that shatters the denial of what is inside. The phrase, "I don't want to get old," is spoken, but the evidence of aging cannot be denied, hidden or turned back. The adult who has not reached emotional maturity will lash out at the aging process and try to control it by reversing and slowing time.

In each circumstance, the midlife spouse feels their life is slipping beyond their control, as steady emotional change continues to sweep over them. All repressed emotional changes seem to break through at once and the insurmountable pressure builds. Fear and rebellion drive them to make drastic and terrible mistakes, as their state of mind collapses into deep confusion and change continues to overtake them.

The Beginning of the Crisis for the Left-behind Spouse

As the stages of a midlife crisis progress, the timing of the emotional bomb[1] dropped on the unsuspecting spouse always occurs in the third stage of the midlife crisis.[2]

Whether uncovered through accidental discovery or through confrontation, the effects are emotionally devastating. These effects herald the beginning of an emotional crisis for the unsuspecting spouse (you), putting you on a road that was not of your own creation.

---

[1] The emotional bomb is the time when the MLC spouse's emotional pressure in Self comes to a boiling point, and it comes out in deep anger, blame, shame and guilt that are projected upon the left behind spouse, and the marriage is sent to its death at that time. This is the time when the journey for the left behind spouse will begin. The midlife spouse will have already entered the third stage. There may or may not be an affair in progress at the time this unwanted emotional bomb drop happens.

[2] The third stage of the crisis is called Emotional Regression.

Just as the crisis of the midlife spouse is their journey to wholeness and emotional healing, the journey of the left-behind spouse is all about your healing. Nothing you do or say is going to change the course of your midlife spouse. Their crisis will continue forward until they resolve it themselves. The midlife spouse must have time, space, and God's help to come through whole and healed. Your intuition is your best guide during this time as you learn to set loving and firm boundaries to influence the midlife spouse to grow up.

There are no shortcuts around this trial. The only way out is through. The only way through, is by facing, resolving, and healing the painful issues of the past that have caused your spouse's midlife crisis. Though you have always been with them, please remember that you did not break them, so you cannot be expected to fix them.

This is an opportunity to redefine you. It is a time of change and growth to become what God purposed. One has the choice to step out of their former ways of acting, thinking and relating and step into the process of emotional maturity. This journey will help you recognize the flaws within and take the necessary steps to repair.[1]

It takes time. Yet, it is never a waste of time when one chooses to move into the personal journey toward a goal of eventual wholeness and healing. As you walk this journey, you will improve and gain understanding within the realm of what has happened and may happen in the future. Time is on your side.

---

[1] If not repaired, these flaws go from relationship to relationship, recycling until the lessons are learned.

Your journey and the journey of the midlife spouse are connected. Emotional maturity and change in one person evokes change in the other. Both spouses have inner work to do, and though the third stage is the longest and hardest to endure, it is also an opportunity for personal growth and healing. If you do not do the inner work, learn and apply the lessons offered,[1] the midlife crisis will not progress forward as intended.

How to use this Book

This first section of this book provides information about the midlife crisis of your spouse and explains the six stages and two healing phases. The second section provides an in-depth look at Stage three of the crisis, Emotional Regression, which is the longest and most damaging phase. The third section is devoted to the subject of the midlife affair, as this is the hardest of the running behaviors for a left-behind spouse to navigate. The final section contains survival skills and life lessons for the left-behind spouse to help on their individual journey toward wholeness and healing. Remember, this journey is all about you. Leave your midlife spouse in the capable hands of God as you move forward.

This book is for your understanding and growth. The spouse in crisis will reject anything you tell them about this journey and will only see your explanations as manipulative and controlling. Below is a clear list of what NOT to tell a spouse in crisis:

---

[1] A complete guide for the left behind spouse is included in this book, which includes some of the life lessons available for you to learn, apply and exercise during this period of life.

- Do NOT say they are in crisis.
- Do NOT share your feelings. This gives them emotional ammunition to fuel justifications for their bad behavior.
- Do NOT say the marriage is dead.
- Do NOT say you are not in love with them.
- Do NOT intentionally speak hurtful things.
- Do NOT return evil for evil.

Encouragement

Be courageous and stay the course. It is human nature to want a reconciled, restored marriage without doing the inner work and standing in the battle for a restored marriage. People are tempted by the path of least resistance, straying from the harder path in favor of thinking there is an easier way.

There is no easier way. Those who do not do the inner work will eventually find themselves in worse trials than before and will repeat this same path. The only difference will be changes in the names, faces and places. The midlife trial will repeat, only worse. *Do what God says do, and all will go well with you.*

No matter what happens, every situation works to the good of those who love the Lord and are called according to His purpose.[1] God's role in this trial is more important than you will ever realize. He absolutely loves you and will continue to work directly and indirectly in your life to convince you of that.

---

[1] Romans 8:28

Chapter 2

For each trial we face, we gain something as a result if we are willing to endure through to the finish line.

Recognizing Growth Scripts

In the last chapter, we reviewed the defined growth patterns followed in maturity. We also discussed how the midlife spouse was confronted with a problem earlier in life that originated on the inside of Self. In this chapter, we relate the script and repressed issues to the period of midlife transition.

Each spouse in crisis tends to speak the same immature language that shows an emotional struggle between right and wrong. They tend to rewrite history in a way that projects the blame for their unhappiness onto their left-behind spouse. They make statements the left-behind spouse has never heard them express about the marriage, their emotions, etc. They also follow a certain script in doing things that are out of character.

Certain behaviors and comments are made by each midlife spouse in crisis, in spite of the differences in circumstances. God has chosen certain "hallmarks" or signs to show similarities and sameness that help identify and clearly recognize when someone is in midlife crisis. Someone who has walked the same road recognizes this script and understands that the midlife spouse[1] is in crisis.

Listed below are the more common hallmarks and signs.

The Hallmarks of the Crisis

- The Emotional Bomb Drop that marks the start of the journey for the left-behind spouse, which includes several ways of saying, "I love you, but I'm not in love with you". This statement shows evidence of deep confusion about their feelings, which had been clear before. (Though this is the beginning of the journey for the left-behind spouse, the midlife spouse has already advanced to stage three of their crisis.)
- The confusion that exists within the realm of their emotions, which shows regardless of what they do. As the crisis moves forward, their confusion moves into many other areas.
- The total withdrawing from the left-behind spouse, both emotionally and physically.
- The mental capacity of the midlife spouse that deteriorates to such an extent they make life changing decisions that spread lasting damage across their families. Some relationships are broken for a lifetime. (This hallmark of the crisis is unseen until the Lord reveals it in full to the left-behind spouse.)
- The running behaviors that can include, but are not limited to, the midlife crisis affair.

---

[1] This also applies to emotionally immature people who are not in a midlife crisis.

- The rebellion that is observed within the midlife spouse against everything they ever believed in, including the left-behind spouse. It also involves a great deal of spewing, confusion, and rewriting of history that deeply confuses the left-behind spouse who knows what they are hearing is not correct.
- The "dark side" versus the "light side" within each midlife spouse who experiences the "opposite behaviors" that are seen.[1] It is a true battle between good and evil.

The Emotional Development Process

The midlife transition that so often transforms into a midlife crisis is an emotional development process, triggered by the death of youth. It is an important part of emotional growth and contains the symptoms of depression, anger, withdrawal, and avoidance, to name a few.

As children are forced into the process of puberty transforming a child into a young adult, the young adult is forced into midlife transition. Midlife transforms a young adult into a middle-aged adult; one that will face the challenges and changes of becoming older.[2]

The death of one's youth is the foremost major issue that all people in midlife are called upon to face and accept. Why? Because it has

---

[1] The "opposite behaviors" are explained further in the book.
[2] And prepare them for eventual death.

everything to do with accepting the aging process in general.[1] In midlife, this issue changes their perception of Self, their lives, families, spouse and marriage, as they struggle to accept the truth.

A midlife crisis is a time of emotional redevelopment humans must face, for changing, growing, and becoming a mature emotional adult. It is a painful internal growth process that begins with the altered perception of one's life that has led them into this place. The midlife spouse's deep emotional pain will be seen very clearly at times.

Explanation of the Stages of the Midlife Crisis

Within the depths of this book, you will learn how a midlife crisis usually begins, how it should end, coping strategies, and hopefully find some measure of peace through the study of these pages.

There are six stages of the crisis and two healing stages that a midlife spouse must go through to finish this process in full. The stages will be navigated in the order of appearance below. Although there will be emotional cycling during this time, this does not mean they have missed or skipped any part of the crisis. These stages are written as a guide to aid in the navigation through your spouse's midlife crisis and are not to be considered an absolute road map. They are presented herein with as complete an expansion as can be provided at this time.

And finally, understand that depression, anger, and withdrawal are

---

[1] I have expounded at length, describing the various aspects seen during this time, and you will see more of these descriptions within the later chapters of this book.

present throughout this entire process, so do not take anything the midlife spouse does or says personally. Their crisis is their problem, it is not about you, and it never was. If you can grasp this one truth, your journey will be easier to step into and navigate.

The Stages of a Midlife Crisis[1]

1. A Change of Perception
2. Loss of Emotional Control
3. Total Emotional Regression
4. Facing Total Failure
5. Introspection
6. The Final Facing
7. The Settling Down Process
8. The Final Inner Healing

Roadmaps and Timelines

Understandably, the left-behind spouse wants roadmaps and timelines to mark progress through the crisis and a shortcut or quick-fix to save the marriage. None are given. No matter what one tries to speed up the process, it will not happen. Any attempt to accelerate will be blocked by the midlife crisis process. The only way out is through.[2]

---

[1] Those of you familiar with my prior writings will find all stages rewritten, and renamed, for simplicity.

[2] God, in His infinite wisdom, has made certain there is no way over, under or around this experience. Since we are His creation, He knows us well, not to mention the various tricks people try in an attempt to avoid the crisis. God is also responsible for the time factor that contributes to the length of the crisis. He set the requirements for completion of this trial and He will be with both spouses through the trial. He could come in any time and heal all issues

I have not included timelines for the stages. Timelines are not set in stone and, if given, tend to raise expectations to an unhealthy degree, as they focus on stopping the process and getting out of the trial as soon as possible. There is no stopping the midlife crisis, as time must work its healing. The length of time from start to finish depends on the one walking the journey, who sets their own timetable. Some in crisis will progress through in as little as four years, others can take twelve or more years to complete the stages.

Not only are there no timelines, but there is also no straight path leading to the end of this journey. The road is filled with hairpin turns, ruts and rocks, and traverses' hills that transform into mountains and dip into valleys. The crisis takes time to navigate and depends on each individual and their willingness to face their issues. The greater the number of past issues and the more painful they are, the longer the crisis will last. Whether a midlife spouse will come through is up to them.

The left-behind spouse works to figure out where their midlife spouse is based on the stages and descriptions herein. Most of what is learned about the crisis occurs in hindsight and there is no marking progress until one can look back and see where the midlife spouse has been. Some may show one stage at a time, while others show more than one. The temptation to fall into the trap of situational acceleration exists, hoping something that has presented indicates the midlife spouse has moved into a new stage. But remember, repetitious emotional cycling accompanies the crisis, and

---

related to the midlife crisis, but He chooses not to do this. Why? Because if He delivered everyone from every trial, there would be no benefit gained. The time spent within any given trial is time well spent learning the lessons given. There is no fast tracking this journey to wholeness and healing.

denial, anger, depression and withdrawal are present throughout the crisis. The crisis will proceed in the order listed above, and there will be no skipping or missing stages.

It is often difficult to keep up with the emotional cycling and the issues the midlife spouse struggles to resolve. For the most part, what one thinks they see is something disguised or hidden under another layer of the journey. People standing on the outside cannot see clearly into the inside of a person, and the situation often reflects different dynamics at different times.

If the crisis is not navigated successfully in full, the individual in crisis will be subjected to consistent negative cycles of emotional crisis for as long as it takes to resolve Self. The process must be navigated in full before the new life commences. As long as issues remain unresolved, the crisis continues. The best thing to do is to leave the midlife spouse with God so He can do His best work. God knows how to get through to even the most stubborn of midlife spouses.

The Role of the Left-behind Spouse

The midlife crisis literally demands completeness. All aspects and issues of both spouses will be resolved in full. Understanding this truth gives the left-behind spouse permission to detach and allow the process to bring about all aspects of facing, growth, change, and becoming whole.

No one has any control over what will happen except the person in crisis. The left-behind spouse will be forced to release the midlife spouse to make their own decisions and put the focus on Self.

This is a hard road and often takes time to begin the first step. It is the journey of a lifetime that will enrich your life, change your attitude, and teach you about Self as well as mature you as God originally meant you to become. But remember, it all takes time.

Encouragement

God does not remain idle during this time. He works quietly in the background, ensuring the journey contains all aspects designed and tailored to the personal transition of both spouses. He knows what makes you tick and what it will take to bring you through this personal trial. He deals with you differently than the midlife spouse, because you are clear thinking while your midlife spouse operates in confusion.

If you choose to stand for your marriage because of love and hope that remain within your heart, pray for your midlife spouse. God works steadily within the heart of your spouse, delving deeply within their very soul in response to your prayers. He nudges them at right times, speaking words of wisdom into their hearts to guide them forward. God watches for the times He can work freely, as these are the times, He does His best work. There is always hope as long as love remains in your heart.

Chapter 3

Sometimes it takes making horrendous mistakes to show that person the error of their ways,
which then leads to change, growth and maturity.

Stages of a Mid-Life Crisis[1]

1. A Change of Perception
2. Loss of Emotional Control
3. Total Emotional Regression
4. Facing Total Failure
5. Introspection
6. The Final Facing
7. The Settling Down Process
8. The Final Inner Healing

Stage 1 | A Change of Perception

At the beginning of the midlife crisis, there are several things subjected to a change of perception. The primary aspect is the fact the midlife spouse is getting older. The secondary aspect is time and the knowledge that it cannot be turned back. In addition, the midlife spouse finds they are on a specific emotional threshold facing the death of their youth. This leads into three realizations:

---

[1] Those of you familiar with my prior writings will find that all stages rewritten, and renamed, for simplicity.

- They are not old, but neither are they young.
- What once was, will never be again.
- Change has begun, they have no choice in the matter, and they have yet to face and understand what this change will reveal.

The slowly dawning realization begins to lead into a new state of self-awareness between the age of 35 and 40. They do not wish to see they are being forced into various physical, mental and emotional changes. In denial, they attempt to push these changes back.

While this is not a fast-dawning situation,[1] it does not help when a major life's event, such as the death of a loved one, facing death personally, or a child graduating from high school, completes this "trigger." Each milestone in life brings them face to face with their current perception of Self. Once triggered, it becomes harder to push back the realization, much like a biological clock sounding an alarm that cannot be turned off.

When their eyes finally open to reality, fear begins to grow. Many consider going the cosmetic route to enhance the illusion of youth. Many more go on a buying spree for a new wardrobe that does not suit their age. Some, thinking material things will help, buy "toys" better suited for the young, such as fast automobiles and motorcycles.

When teased about getting older, they laugh, but negatively internalize the comments. They realize they do not have the same energy and physical endurance as before. They look at their children from the view of this changing perception and see them as still being young. By contrast, the children are teenagers going

---

[1] This situation is often gradual.

through puberty, standing on the threshold of young adulthood. From this same changed perception, mired in the past, the midlife spouse attempts to treat their teenagers as they did when they were younger. The teenager rebels against being treated like a young child. This state of ordinary rebellion by the pubescent teenager increases the confusion of the midlife spouse, who tries to make up for lost time, only to find rejection from their teenagers. Though their feelings are hurt, the midlife spouse reacts in a controlling way. Their frustration from failed expectations translates into anger.

Last, but never least, the spouse of the midlife individual does not look the same as before. Of course, as the midlife spouse has aged over time, so has their mate. The effect heredity has on one's looks cannot be helped. However, their spouse is a direct reflection of them, how they have treated them, what they have given or withheld over the course of a long-term marriage, and the midlife spouse begins to turn from what they see.

They think, "If I had it to do all over, I may have married someone else and been happier." This is a false perception. But as they reflect, they are led down a road of deep resentment which simmers under the surface.

They have a desire and strong temptation to run from everything. Their minds cross into deep dissatisfaction, they become restless, and reality intrudes upon the denial they lived in. Their first reaction is to develop extremely skewed thinking, which reveals itself in time as their emotional crisis gets under way. Everything within dissolves into chaotic confusion. A mental, emotional and spiritual storm has begun. No one knows what the midlife spouse is thinking, they only see that the midlife spouse has become withdrawn as the result of a highly active mind.

The midlife spouse does not talk, so no one knows what is occurring until the next stage begins. If asked, they say they are fine, but if one listens closely, their answers are spoken through annoyance. What they really want is to be left alone to think about everything.

Stage 2 | Loss of Emotional Control

While the midlife spouse is within the prior stage, grappling with changes beyond their understanding, they are in preparation for this next stage. These various changes ready them for the next set of events, and the emotional pressure built during their change of perception begins to reveal itself.

As resentment builds within, specific and undeniable realities become known, and the midlife spouse reacts angrily at their lot in life. Self-absorption takes over, as they forget others face the same problems. Nothing matters except Self - how they feel, and how they wrongly perceive they have been used and abused throughout their life.

In selfishness, they act indifferent to how they hurt the people closest to them. If questioned about their resentful and angry behavior, they cannot answer why they feel the way they do. They lash out at their supervisors at work, not caring if their wrong attitude causes them to lose their job. Their irritability increases, and they react with more resentment that leads to an even deeper anger. They do not understand why they are angry and resentful, but they continue, as their emotions take precedence over everything and everyone that once mattered to them.

They say they are speaking and acting out how they feel for the first time in their lives. They feel they have given everything they can and now is the time to do for themselves. They do not care how anyone else feels about their attitude. As their anger is worn on their sleeve, they act out overtly, walking over anyone who stands in their way.

The midlife spouse continues down this destructive road and thinks more about running away. Their resentment increases because of their wrongly skewed perception that they are stuck. They deeply resent the fact their children have grown up without them, and their spouse is not what they think he/she should be.

Their resentment increases exponentially, as they feel life has dealt them a cruel blow. Within their constantly changing perception, the midlife spouse becomes deeply angry, feeling trapped in a life that has become unsatisfying and empty. Everything comes together as it dawns on them, they are growing older. No matter what they do, the aging process continues inexorably forward.

As they continue to dwell on these deeply resentful feelings, they think of ways to fix this perceived problem. "If they could change their life, they would be happy." But even the thought of change scares them. They look for outside sources to blame for the unhappiness they feel inside, and eventually they lash out at the one person who has always been there - their spouse.

The outward expression of their deeply felt resentment takes the beginning form of small criticisms. These gradually increase until the midlife spouse emotionally spins out of control. The least thing triggers a dramatic emotional explosion. In time, these emotionally explosive episodes transform into strong tantrums, as the midlife spouse makes impossible demands.

Their mate walks on emotional eggshells. The departure of the married couples' former life becomes more defined. They barely speak without a fight breaking out from the "sane" spouse saying or doing the wrong things.

As the emotional door into the next stage begins to open, the increasingly resentful and angry outbursts from the midlife spouse (and the negative reaction that comes from their mate), feeds their justification and reasoning for every destructive act they perpetrate.

Trying to make themselves feel better about their perceived lot in life, some find a friend outside of marriage. In the process of making an emotional connection, which never goes below the surface, they do not know the new friendship may become the out-of-control midlife affair.

Others abuse drugs or alcohol, continuing their quest for youth, and engaging in their search for self-identity. As time moves forward, the increasing anger, resentment, and emotional pressure that are consistently building, progress toward an inevitable explosion.

Without warning, within the mind of the midlife spouse, everything within their lives, (including their marriage that had served them faithfully for many years), dies a sudden death. At that point, the midlife spouse sets everything in their current life aside to begin the emotional crossover into the next stage.

Through this same door, they will directly face the past they have not resolved within themselves. As they continue crossing over, they show very clear signs of total emotional regression.

Stage 3 | Total Emotional Regression

The third stage, seen as the peak, falls in the middle of the crisis.

The midlife spouse attempts to use outside sources to fix their inside problems. The first (and worst) of their past emotional issues surface not long after they come into this stage. Because they cannot and will not face the fact they are truly broken within, they run. Their rebellious antics, which began during the last stage, become worse as full emotional regression takes over.

If you keep an open mind and pay attention, the "children"[1] of the midlife spouse's past issues are viewed clearly and interacted with more directly. These certain-aged children tell their past story in pieces, using projection and angry confused spewing to bring it forth. They continue searching for what they perceive was lost when they faced the actual death of their youth, not realizing they can never regain what has gone into the past. They search for outside sources to blame for their misery and try anything as they attempt to avoid the necessary confrontation of Self. In addition, the painful issues of their past relentlessly pursue them.

Because the midlife spouse probably began an emotional connection during the prior stage, it is possible for this friendship to progress into an emotional or physical connection. This usually creates the foundation for the midlife affair. Even though they know this connection is wrong, the midlife spouse does everything they can to stop their pain. As they progress deeper into the fires of the crisis, worse emotional damage occurs.

During this time, they become the total opposite[2] of who they were before they entered the life-changing process of the midlife crisis. As total regression goes into a mental and emotional rewind, they gradually change from what they were to the direct opposite. This

---

[1] A more complex explanation can be found in the chapter entitled, "The Children of their Issues".
[2] More about Opposite Behaviors in Section 3, Running Behaviors of MLC

opposite behavior clearly shows.

If they were distant from their children in the past, they try to connect with their children. If they were connected to their children, they disconnect or distance from them. If they were non-confrontational, they become direct and blunt. If they were quiet, they become talkative. If they were mild-mannered, patient people, they become irritable, on edge, and extremely impatient. Becoming the opposite means they become a person the left-behind spouse either has not known before, or used to know, but no longer remembers or recognizes. Most midlife spouses do things their husbands/wives never thought they would do.

The midlife spouse shows entitlement behaviors, thinking they deserve what they take, regardless of whom they hurt or the financial bind they cause their family. Their reasoning becomes, "I spent my life doing what everyone wanted me to do. Now, it is my turn, and no one can stop me."

Their emotions increase in ways never experienced, as emotional-thinking and decision-making overrun logical thinking. The midlife spouse does not understand the forces driving them down this painful emotional road. As a result, they panic and run. Their various types of running rock and destroy the very foundation of their marriage. One of the major issues is a quest to find their lost identity, and they wander through an emotional wilderness of rebellion. Nothing will satisfy them for very long, if at all.

Many midlife spouses question the existence of God and often turn away from Him. Many more fall into various temptations and possibly have one or several affairs. Because they continue to distance themselves from their actions, they fail to see their wrongdoing. The midlife spouse is deeply lost in the entitlement attitude called, "It is my time now."

The emotional bomb is dropped during this time, shocking their spouse.[1] The existing problems escalate, as the emotionally devastated spouse cries, begs, and pleads. At this point, the transition goes into full-blown crisis. As the marital situation deteriorates, the midlife spouse turns away, secure in the various justifications for wrong behaviors. Their rebellious behavior can disrupt the most settled of families, especially the midlife affair. The midlife spouse's emotional reasoning is such they think they have found the emotional connection they once lost.

As this stage continues to progress, there is a marked change observed within the midlife spouse's energy levels. Higher levels of energy are expended during the running behaviors. The high energy aspect includes, but is not limited to, the self-medicating behaviors they show within the midlife affair, the abusing of drugs and alcohol, or spending money.

The high energy shown during the peak, or height of this stage, is comparable to a fully inflated balloon rising out of control. Every midlife spouse shows this high level of energy at some point during this stage. Signs are shown through tantrums thrown when confronted with a boundary or they trigger Self into whirlwind bouts of angry and confused spewing. (The anger must come from inside out and it shows in this high energy display.) Most left-behind spouses do not recognize the high level of energy, or they do not see it because the midlife spouse has moved out.

---

[1] The unwanted emotional bomb is not the beginning of the midlife spouse's emotional journey. By the time the left behind spouse becomes aware something is seriously wrong, the midlife spouse has been on their journey for a while. However, there is a true purpose in this triggered awareness, for it is the beginning of the journey for the left behind spouse toward their own wholeness and healing.

In time, reality leads to truth and intrudes upon their time of fantasy, which puts a cramp in their high-energy antics. Because all affairs are constructed upon an unstable emotional foundation comprised of dishonesty, deceit, and secrecy, the midlife spouse eventually finds the affair partner, with whom they can/will get involved, is not what they wanted. However, they will not see any of this until they experience an emotional awakening that shows them a change of direction.

First Emotional Awakening

The first emotional awakening serves to bring the midlife spouse into the realization that change continues to pressure them forward. This should start them along the path toward facing their issues, opening the door for a time of a deeper depression, as their various failures come to light.

As this awakening, progresses, their emotional awareness increases. Despite how they may try to avoid this growing awareness, the ongoing pressure to move forward increases until they are finally forced into the downhill slide leading toward the crossover into the next stage.

The midlife spouse who returns home always does so during this stage. They return broken, have already awakened, and their ongoing internal struggles become clearer. The left-behind spouse will see an extremely exhausted, tired, and deeply depressed midlife spouse. The exhaustion and depression continue to deepen as the midlife spouse continues preparing for the crossover into the next stage. Though they may still have times of confusion and rebellious behavior, they show a clear line of emotional separation from the left-behind spouse, which is typical.

The third stage is the longest of the stages, depending on the rebellious and self-medicating behaviors used. Because this stage is the longest and hardest for the left-behind spouse to endure, the remainder of the book focuses on the emotions, aspects, and other issues one is likely to see within their midlife spouse, as well as life lessons and survival skills for the left-behind spouse and their own journey to wholeness and healing.

Stage 4 | Facing Total Failure

Fully navigated, the first three stages are now complete. However, until now, the issues inside the midlife spouse have not been faced, nor acknowledged. During this stage, the midlife spouse begins to directly face the issues from which they cannot turn away. They feel as though they are a complete and total failure.

They suffer serious regret because nothing they have done has helped during those first three stages. Everything they have tried has resulted in utter failure, and now comes the time to face their damage. All facing is done on the inside, because their already-present depression deepens even more. The anger that spewed outward so readily before now turns inward. Their self-esteem is destroyed, and they feel as if nothing they have ever done was right. They wonder whether they are worth anything to anyone.

Physical changes related to aging cause their hormones to imbalance and fluctuate. This only makes them feel worse. Some midlife spouses suffer through so much emotional pain, they commit suicide, while some decide to see a doctor. Antidepressants will help but will remove just enough of the emotional confusion for the midlife spouse to cope with daily life. The issues will remain to be faced, resolved, and healed. Some suffer in silence, thinking nobody understands what they are going through.

They are on the verge of tears (or cry all the time), constantly pacing the floor, losing sleep, afraid of what they perceive is in the dark. No matter what they do, they are unable to escape negative thoughts, cutting themselves down in word and action. Extreme guilt and shame may compound this stage. Because there is so much internal pressure, they become forgetful and often irritable. At other times, they want to be left alone, becoming very argumentative and sometimes unresponsive. They may disappear for lengthy periods continuing to take their space as needed, or they may spend much time playing mindless computer games, watch a lot of television, and starring into space.

The physical signs after hitting rock bottom are: neglected physical hygiene, tears, and being unsteady on their feet. They may berate Self repeatedly, but remember, they are still seeing the first part of the damage they have caused, which was shown when they awakened within the last stage.

This is the deepest emotional pit of the midlife crisis and is extremely difficult for them. However, if they fight hitting rock bottom, they can become stuck as they desperately cycle backward for a time, then forward. Each cycle backward becomes more painful than the last, as God takes a hand in this and begins driving the midlife spouse forward into this necessary place.

For the left-behind spouse, this is a frightening time because they want to help. However, they cannot make the midlife spouse receive help. As a matter of fact, as the midlife spouse continues to slide downward, they refuse all help. In time, they hit the emotional rock bottom within the throes of this very deep depression. Staying at rock bottom grows extremely uncomfortable. The longer they languish in this state, the more painful it becomes, because the midlife spouse is not meant to stay in this position.

After this difficult landing, they discover two choices: *Stay where they are in their misery or climb out.* Increasing pain is the motivator that gets them moving, because the only way out is up. Once they climb out, they move into another emotional change that shifts their perception, which assists them into the next stage of Introspection.

You must understand they will come through this, or they will not. No one can make them come out until they are ready. Pestering or pushing them will only cause them to emotionally withdraw. They need the continued space to work within Self. During this time, they are trying to understand some of what has happened in the parts they can face. These parts involve resolving issues inside them, from childhood and other parts of their past. Understand, this journey must continue to be walked alone, because no one can fix this or do it for them.

Clear signs of an even deeper emotional withdrawal begin to come to the fore as each issue is faced, resolved, and healed. A gradual slide from Facing Total Failure to Introspection occurs, or both stages can occur in tandem. If both stages combine, one observes the deepened depression mixed with the introspective aspect. In time, the depressive aspect gradually recedes, leaving the introspective processing. When and how they navigate forward is still up to them, as it always was.

Stage 5 | Introspection

For the first time during the crisis, the midlife spouse faces the personal, self-related issues they have avoided. These issues may come all at once or singularly. The midlife spouse faces the problems deep within their psyche that influenced the damage done in stage three.

As each past issue is fully examined and processed, major decisions are made by the midlife spouse in the aspects of job, life, past relationships, spouse, and marriage.

There is one other aspect to consider:

As the midlife spouse begins this time of deep processing, the Archway of the Final Fears comes into view. The stage of Introspection is an open emotional field, designed to be navigated with little hindrance. However, this stage also contains a temptation to try to move ahead, because the goal or the exit (The Final Fears) is in plain sight.

During this time, one of three things will occur:

- The midlife spouse continues rebuilding the once-destroyed connections, while completing the processing needed to help them reach the final stage of their crisis.
- They withdraw completely and rebel against what they know must be done for and within Self.
- They attempt to avoid or skip this whole stage, and most of the next, in favor of reaching their Final Fears so they may come out of this process more quickly.

The third option will not work because this process will not allow any aspect of the midlife crisis to be avoided or skipped. If the midlife spouse tries to go directly from the beginning of this stage into the Archway that leads into the Final Fears, they are immediately locked out. Thus, the midlife spouse is emotionally recycled to the beginning of Introspection where they must begin this part of the process again. It becomes all or none, and what is not learned is consistently recycled until the lessons are fully learned. Each time a recycling is done, the emotional road becomes harder to walk and a sense of déjà vu begins to occur.

Because all processing is done inwardly, much of it is difficult to discern. It is advisable to continue leaving the midlife spouse alone in their processing, unless guided by intuition into one of two aspects:

- Pushing the midlife spouse forward, triggering an outward spewing of deep anger that will help clear their mind.
- The midlife spouse triggers themselves into an emotional tantrum designed to clear their minds and help gain clarity.

Otherwise, the left-behind spouse would most likely see a gradual clearing of the midlife spouse's countenance (facial expression). Each time a major decision is made, a lessening of stress should be observed.

Over time, a gentler person slowly emerges. At first, that might bring confusion, because it is all too easy to mistake the end of this stage for the beginning of the next one. Some midlife spouses go on to finish the facing of their past issues in full during this time. Others may finish some issues but carry some forward for further processing. Each person is different in how they deal with this stage.

Just as the first four stages have been overt, this one stage is mostly covert. It is subject to continued deep introspection and inner processing as they consider the beginning of what will either be the end, or a new beginning within their lives at this point.

Shades of the first four stages may still be seen within their deep struggles. In addition, it is clearly discovered that the husband/wife the midlife spouse abandoned at the beginning of the third stage will become a major part of the issues they must also figure out for Self.

There is a choice to stay or leave. For a time, a concentrated effort will be made to influence the left-behind spouse to end the marriage. As difficult as it is, the left-behind spouse is encouraged to continue standing, and lead the midlife spouse forward, gently but firmly, even as the struggle within is observed.

This stage contains a clear preview of future behavior leading into the final stage. Eventually, the midlife spouse should choose to accept their jobs, lives, past relationships, spouse, and finally recommit to their marriage. These decisions, once made, help them cross into the final stage.

Major keys that will end Introspection:

- Showing a full understanding of what they did, knowing when it started, and why it happened.
- No longer blaming their spouse for damage done to the marriage by the midlife spouse.
- Exercising proper commitment to the marriage and choosing the left-behind spouse.
- Explaining Self in full.
- Showing apologetic behavior.
- Making changes that reflect their future growth.

If the midlife spouse balks at any time because of fear and does not complete the major decisions faced, they will remain in this stage. The only way out is through.

The Process of Creating Space for Change, Growth and Becoming

Once the business of issue-facing begins in earnest, the midlife spouse realizes there is an empty space to be filled that replaces the vacuum they once felt. As their individual issues are cleared and the various pieces come together, they find more room to recreate Self.

It's extremely painful, yet positively challenging. Their renewed strength rises to meet the final obstacles that must be cleared to create this positive space within their heart. No one can fill this space except the person who created it. Once they complete all changes, they begin the task of settling down. This involves exploring the new aspects within Self that are a result of the long journey into their own wholeness and healing. This phase stretches into the Settling Down Process where everything is put into its emotional place.

Stage 6 | The Final Facing

Under normal circumstances, the midlife spouse settles all personal issues before they enter this final stage. However, it is not uncommon nor unusual for a midlife spouse to carry a few issues into this first phase of the last stage. The ability to handle this last stage depends on the left-behind spouse's willingness to walk this journey for Self, because it connects with the midlife spouse's journey more closely than realized, even to the point of going through various positive changes.

The Final Facing stage is navigated in a series of three phases:

Phase 1: The Final Disintegration

This phase involves the complete disintegration of the personality of the midlife spouse. This is done in preparation of complete death to self, which will come later. This will eventually lead into a full reintegration which is a necessary part of the rebirth to Self, achieved during the Final Fears.

The veil is lifted, showing the midlife spouse everything, no holds barred. This is better described as the chemical change within the brain that began just before they went into full emotional regression and triggered their depression. It is the sole foundation for the midlife crisis fog. The midlife spouse realizes for the first time the damage done to their life, marriage, and spouse. Their spouse will be surprised to see more children surface, as well as flashes of the old personality, new personality, as well as good and bad personalities.

This takes on the appearance of suffering from multiple personalities. But considering they are still literally in pieces, or disintegrated, they connect deeper with their core Self rather than covering it with layers of justification as previously done. This veil-lifting process is a time of necessary facing and deeper processing that must be completed before moving out of this part of the emotional crisis.

The Second Emotional Awakening

This is the second awakening within the midlife crisis. Clarity of thought is restored, depression, withdrawal, and anger are lifted. Though they may still show the children aspect, their emotional strength increases. They must go through this as part of their preparation for the last third of the crisis, their Final Fears. Without this added clarity and the attaining of emotional strength, they would be unable to face what awaits them much later. This clarity and emotional strength increases as they continue navigating through this final stage.

The process of the midlife crisis was designed to extract a permanent change that continues to lead into change, growth and becoming within the midlife spouse. This final disintegration process forces them to look at every facet of their personalities and make permanent changes. The key to helping them through is to accept what you see as it comes forth. Do not ridicule or shame them. Try to understand them in a truly compassionate fashion. True and Godly remorse may or may not appear during this time. However, they will apologize for everything they can think of and try to make up for the damage done.

Phase 2: The Final Temptations

During this phase, the final set of temptations will be revealed that test their emotional strength and resolve. The silence, patience and understanding of the left-behind spouse is most important during this time, as they must come through alone. They will appear to move backward, which is necessary in moving forward. It is during this time they appear to revisit all stages of the crisis except the first one and they shut the door to each stage permanently one by one, never to return. Some people have missing pieces[1] that must be gathered and resolved. They will emotionally cycle back to retrieve those to continue this ongoing process of putting Self back together.

As they go through this necessary process of shutting these various doors, Satan will tempt them. To them what is ahead seems harder than what lies behind. The path of least resistance will be shown one final time. During this time, as they draw upon their newly found strength to overcome this aspect, they learn a major lesson: Temptation will always lurk around every corner. The question will always remain: Do you walk away from temptation or fall into it? They learn everyone has the choice to stand or fall.

This temptation remains until they pass through the door leading out of the storm that began their crisis. If they should give in to the temptation to go backward instead of progressing forward, they will emotionally cycle backward. However, they can only cycle back to stages where the doors have not been permanently closed. Most of the time they are only allowed to cycle back to the last stage but will continue the process of moving forward as they feel emotionally safe. They must be allowed to come through without interruption, no matter what happens.

Within this same aspect of closing doors forever, there are midlife spouses who end their midlife affair during the third stage and have no further addiction or feeling for the former affair partner. However, they can, and do, suffer guilt and shame over how they mistreated the affair partner when the affair broke down. This is not the same aspect as having the misplaced responsibility they showed when the affair ended. It is part of the humanitarian aspect within them that returns to be seen. Regardless of the sin committed,

---

[1] For more information, refer to "Jigsaw Puzzle Analogy" in Section 2, Emotional Cycling.

treating anyone like they are less than nothing is shameful. The midlife spouse sees this as they are continuing to shut their respective doors for good. It is not uncommon for them to think to check on the former affair partner, to make sure they are okay, and it is tempting to do so. Some may call, some may visit, and some may simply stand still and fight to overcome this remaining guilt and shame arising from past mistreatment of the affair partner.

If the above behaviors are not seen, one may see the prior actions temporarily return, like running for the phone when it rings, clearing the caller ID, struggling within Self to settle past damage committed while within the midlife affair. Or one may see none of this. Every situation is different, but any leftover aspects within this major damage done must be settled within Self so this door can be shut. However, they are at the point of knowing and understanding this aspect cannot happen again, and they know their commitment lies with their spouse. They have learned that the outside solution of the long-past affair did not solve the problem that was within Self.

To clear up any misconceptions about this phase: This does not involve a return to the full-blown aspect of the third stage but only a permanent shutting of that door. The mistake of the past midlife affair, if it existed within the third stage, calls for a major processing in this area, so give them as much space as possible. Rest with the realization that the end of their midlife crisis is near.

In summary, this involves the battle concerning the temptation within the aspect of returning to a perceived easier time within the crisis. Nothing more, nothing less. Trust in God and yourself, because nothing is ever as it seems, most especially during a still ongoing major midlife crisis.

Process of Re-bonding

As soon as all doors to the prior stages are closed and temptation is overcome, it is time to reattach the emotional and spiritual bond that was broken between the couple when the midlife spouse destroyed the marriage. Either person can send the request, but most of the time, the midlife spouse is the one who sends while the left-behind spouse receives. This process causes nausea within both people and the average time of finishing this re-bonding is usually four to six hours. In people who do not recognize what is happening, it can take as long as two weeks.

Exiting the Midlife Storm

Once this phase ends, the emotional clouds clear, and the midlife spouse navigates Self out of the midlife crisis storm that heralded their entrance into the crisis. As this exit occurs, the midlife spouse begins searching their soul for the answers that have always been within. At this point, they are clear of their emotional crisis that plagued them for so long. The midlife crisis script ends at this point. Their minds are no longer disoriented and confused, and their perceptions are no longer skewed, distorted, nor overlaid with weakness. Their actions and words come together, and they speak and act from a much better emotional place, showing clarity of mind.

As these inner answers are clearly revealed, the midlife spouse experiences a sense of being driven toward something unknown. Though they experience fear and uncertainty, they have clarity of thought. There are no signs of depression or withdrawal. Though there may be signs of anger, their emotional strength will be seen as never before.

Heavy emotional stress is present during this time. However, the soon-to-be former midlife spouse does not run from what is ahead. If they appear to back off temporarily, it is because they have not fully emerged from the midlife storm. However, once they enter in through the Archway leading into the process of The Final Fears, they cannot turn back. The only way out will be straight through, and the only way through will be to face this final aspect in full.

Phase 3: The Final Fears

This process involves the Archway, or entrance point, which heralds the entry to their final fears. All this time, the midlife spouse has been navigating across this open emotional field, heading toward this archway, where their final fears are located.

During this time, the midlife spouse gathers their remaining emotional strength as they go through a process of preparation. When they are ready, they are guided into the full process of facing the final fears that are exclusive only to them.

Once through the door, there is no going back. No further choice will be given except to navigate this final process in full, moving them through to the other side, before walking through the exit to begin the first of two complete healing processes. Once completely out of the Final Fears, the now former midlife spouse will not be allowed to return. That door closes and locks behind them.

The final fears will vary according to each midlife spouse. No two people are alike, and as each person is different, each midlife process is different. They must overcome their final fears in full or remain in this final process until they do. However, they are never allowed to become stuck in the final fears; it would cause extreme damage within their psyche.

God works in a mighty way to help them navigate through, because

He knows the human mind and emotions could not take this kind of pressure for long. He helps them directly face their final fears for Self. It is a very draining emotional time, and it would not be unusual for their spouse to see darkness in their eyes or on their faces. This is usually a short-lived seeing, there one moment, gone the next.

They will complain of mental and emotional fatigue and often move as if they are filled with lead. They may show intermittent outbursts of emotion and say things that surprise you. The midlife spouse will make cryptic comments that will make you aware they know they have been through something, but they will not be able to name what it is. They will only experience the urgency dictating they get through. Once finished, there will be a positive change in them that is unmistakably peaceful.

The process within the Final Fears is a spiritual, emotional, and mental journey of total transformation from the old Self into the new Self. While in this process, the midlife spouse will face and overcome the greatest fears of their lives. They will first endure complete Death to Self, reducing them into a shade of their former Self.

Next, Judgment is rendered, and afterward, complete Rebirth into a new Self is experienced, leading toward the final exit. The transformed spouse rejoins their spouse on the other side in a completely new way. The two paths become one, leading into the unknown future.

Once the midlife spouse has exited this finished process, Satan is removed so the process of renewal, rebuilding, and reconciliation begin as the Settling Down Process, and then the Final Inner Healing begin. The worst is behind, and the positive changes continue within as they move forward.

Not long after coming out of the final facing and stepping into the first stage of healing, they experience a final rebelling. Once overcome, they have a greater sense of peace replacing the chaos experienced while in crisis. This aspect is much like a teenager who has passed across the threshold into adulthood. There are still final changes that must be made, especially for the one who has done so much damage during the crisis itself. Onward and upward, they move into the first of the healing stages - the Settling Down Process.

Chapter 4

In order to learn to embrace permanent change, one must first experience deep pain.

Stage 7 | The Settling Down Process

Once the Final Fears are exited, a point of settling down follows. This prepares them for two healing processes that result in becoming who God intends them to be. The first healing process is known as the Settling Down Process. Not long before this happens, the midlife spouse completes the process known as Death to the Old Self that leads to Rebirth of the New Self, which leads to a New Beginning portion of the journey.

Those who have exited the crisis find themselves in the need of healing. Their lives, and the lives of others, have sustained mild to severe emotional damage, depending upon the events that occurred during the third stage of the crisis. Whether married or unmarried, everyone has outward damage to heal before their inward damage can hope to reach healing.

For a time, all emotional and spiritual energy is turned inward, and some self-healing is started before helping to heal their loved ones. Because they finished the crisis in full, an emotionally mature adult now stands in the place where the various issue-related children once stood. These same children that ruled their crisis for so long were, in part, responsible for the damage that occurred during that time. However, once resolved in full, the whole of the responsibility lies completely upon the emotionally mature adult.

This newly emerged adult is also responsible for mending fences broken during their emotional crisis. They stand for a time to survey the damage ahead and behind. When ready, with or without help, they begin repairing the damage they know they have caused. Their awareness has long since given way to clarity. They are now strong enough to take whatever negativity comes as they struggle forward within this first healing phase, which will not be an easy task. Though emotionally mature within some aspects, other aspects[1] need completing, eventually assisting them in their quest to reach full emotional maturity. Although largely pieced together by this time, other pieces found during the recent crisis have yet to be fitted into the complete picture of their emotional lives.

During this time, they face people who show them anger and unforgiveness, seeking to punish them for their past transgressions. Others show love and forgiveness, and still others show indifferent and uncaring attitudes. Yet, the newly emerged adult continues forward, taking the time necessary to complete this first phase of their self-healing. They continue facing issues that require resolution, but they will not lash out at others as they did in the past. If lashing out does occur, it is followed immediately by an apology.

As further evidence their dealings with life have changed, they will show patience, tolerance, love, a deeper understanding and a desire to help others. This replaces their prior aspects of entitlement, shallowness, and self-consumption with their wants and desires. This steady metamorphosis results in a gentler personality, one more welcoming than the abrasive, brash, and rebellious personality evidenced during the past fires of the crisis.

As they move forward, the emotional imbalance that led them into the transition will, in time, lead to a complete emotional balance, as they work toward the last and final phase of healing. Just as the

---

[1] These aspects are unique to each individual.

crisis did not come upon them overnight, healing will take time to complete, and goes in step. When one phase is complete, the next remains to be completed.

Post Crisis: The Couple Aspect

To avoid confusion, this section reads from the vantage point of the husband who has newly emerged from the crisis, having rejoined to his wife. This process requires the joint efforts of husband and wife to complete in full, before arriving at the final point of the journey into wholeness and healing.

Although individual in process, there will be times when both spouses are heavily involved in helping one another. Change and growth have occurred throughout the final stage, and eventually, this process brings the couple to the aspect in which their individual paths, separated during the time of the crisis, become one path moving toward a brighter future.

As time advances, the crisis itself becomes outdated, and a bright future lies ahead. During this time, some unresolved issues remain within both the newly emerged husband and the once left-behind spouse. However, instead of working apart, the couple works together toward a common goal, which consists of the final healing process that includes the renewal, reconciliation and rebuilding of a new foundation to augment their new marriage.

During this time, the couple works individual and together, within various aspects unique to their relationship. There will be times of unresolved aspects brought forth by one or the other, placing these upon the proverbial table for marital examination and final resolution.

Clarity comes for both spouses as this aspect continues. The newly emerged husband, through the continuation of his own journey, gains a clearer and changing perception in regard to the past damage he has caused. In that process, he takes complete responsibility for what was done.

Although honest remorse may have shown during the final facing stage, it would not be out of the ordinary for a newly emerged husband to show this aspect for the first time during the Settling Down Process. Given time, the newly emerged husband will speak, guardedly at first, of the feelings experienced during the recent crisis, watching carefully to see how his wife reacts. In the absence of negative reaction, the husband becomes more comfortable opening to his wife, as he feels safe to do so.

The newly emerged husband has many wounds to help heal within his spouse and family. He seeks to further mend all fences broken during the deepest parts of his crisis. Through his wife, he will reach further understanding of how deeply he has damaged his marriage. He will continue to seek for ways to repair these aspects in order to help rebuild this new marriage upon a new foundation.

On the other hand, the wife will continue resolving her individual issues within, as she tries to understand the emotional place her husband speaks from. It will be difficult for her to comprehend what he is saying, and she will suffer from hurt feelings because she is still coming to terms with some things her husband did during his crisis.

In some aspects, it will take the husband to help his wife heal, and in other aspects, it will take the wife to help her husband heal. Outlining clear steps is not possible, as each couple's road into renewal, reconciliation, and rebuilding is vastly different. As each couple is different, each renewal and reconciliation or rebuilding is different. Each couple must find their own way in their own time, which can become lengthy as the couple struggles with past negative feelings. But if each is willing to meet the other halfway, it will eventually work out. Given time, the couple will reach a deeper understanding and the road toward healing will become more easily navigated. Though not easy, this is doable. With the help of the Lord, and the cooperation of both people, the process will complete, leading into the next and final aspect of healing, The Final Inner Healing.

Stage 8 | The Final Inner Healing

After all aspects of the Settling Down Process are completed, the newly emerged emotionally mature adult moves into the Final Inner Healing. This event lasts six months, no more, no less; this is the only specific time in the entire process.

Just before this final process occurs, the post-crisis individual experiences a short time of self-imposed isolation. They stop communicating and show clear signs of withdrawal. This is nothing to be concerned about, as they must process the prior recent experience to be better prepared for this final healing process. However, once their preparation is complete, they move forward with confidence to finish.

Whether single or married, each person's final process is largely the same, although circumstances vary based on each situation. Long before this time, they have stopped running from accountability, and their emotional strength has increased to the point they do not turn away from this challenge.

Emotional maturity increases as they become more than willing to account for Self and their actions of the past. However, there may still be times of deep emotional struggle, as reality continues to shine its light of truth within their psyche. Emotional maturation will continue in various forms and aspects. As the process continues, the last several pieces needed to complete the entire emotional process are finally pieced into their proper places.

As each final aspect is resolved inwardly, the result shows outwardly. Because of this complete renovation within their heart and mind, they embrace change and growth, anticipating what God means for them to become.

Their perception and perspective become more direct, focused, and future oriented. Their giving nature toward others becomes includes love, care, increased tolerance, and a greater patience, without expectations. These are positives within one who has reached full emotional maturity.

Most importantly, they are learning mature love, having learned through this experience that choosing to love deeply involves a sacrifice. Furthermore, when one loves, surrendering of Self is often the result. In this process of learning, they choose to serve others in a real capacity. As God continues to work His hand within, growth overcomes any leftover negative aspects.

Relationships with family and friends renew and strengthen as they apply all they have learned. A monumental task containing various degrees and times of difficulty; yet they rise to this challenge with grace and humility, willing to make amends for the past transgressions committed. Their focus flows outward to help others in their healing, while continuing their healing process within.

Although the Settling Down Process involves helping their loved ones close and heal the wounds directly inflicted while within the midlife crisis, this aspect also involves healing the self-inflicted wounds sustained during outward rebellion.

In explanation, when a person is going through the main part of the midlife crisis, they give the appearance of turning against their spouse (if one exists), family, friends, and all who know and love them. Though rebellion is directed outward, serious emotional damage occurs inwardly. When one hurts others intentionally, or unintentionally, they hurt themselves more. Each hurtful word and act turned outward becomes an inward strike and a self-inflicted emotional betrayal against the moral code they followed before the crisis.

These inward strikes caused the most damage, because these are the sins committed against Self, and the hardest to overcome. Self-forgiveness becomes difficult, because one can more easily forgive others than Self.

A most painful process involves the examination of each emotional betrayal committed against their inner Self. Each resolved issue takes them closer to the point of self-forgiveness, setting the stage for a peaceful and deeply fulfilling life.

Within the married aspect of this necessary process, they continue helping their spouse heal any wounds that remain, even at this late date. Their awareness sharpens, and times of true remorse can still occur. They continue the process of cleaning up the chaos they created in their life, and in the lives of their spouse and family.

As these inner wounds continue to heal, they grieve for what they could have done, but did not do. This is a necessary part of healing these wounds, whether these are contained within or inflicted outwardly. However, since they are continuing the process of helping their spouse and others heal, this grieving period does not last long before their outlook takes another positive direction toward a deeper and final settling aspect within Self.

As the couple works within the process of the reconciliation and rebuilding of their marriage, they continue to work closely together to resolve all issues resulting from the recent experience of the crisis. Because of the couple's joint effort to heal their reconnected marital bond, a scar will eventually replace this earlier wound.

As stated earlier, there are no written steps to help the married couples reconcile and rebuild their broken marriage. Resources exist that can help. However, because the marital dynamics of each marriage differ, it is enough to say that if both have individually taken the journey to wholeness and healing in full, they should contain all necessary tools within to aid one another within these reconciliation and rebuilding phases.

Every marriage that has transcended the midlife crisis is a different type of success. The marital aspect is separate from the completion of the individual journey into wholeness and healing. People often make the mistake of seeing the success of the marriage as the primary goal, not the secondary goal.

To have and support a happy and healthy marriage beyond this point, the journey should be complete for husband and wife. A successful relationship does not depend on one person. Marriage takes two committed, emotionally healthy people willing to do the work of maintenance.

One last thing to note: There are no obvious signs of an ending, no single Fourth of July firework. But life and marriage will be transformed for both individuals. Eventually, all memories in both people purge, and in time will no longer be present. Indeed, time does heal all wounds leading into a peaceful existence.

One Midlife Crisis, Different Possibilities

Marital covenant or not, every married person has the freedom to walk away from their marriage, break their vows and destroy their families. Not every person who faces this monumental life's trial will finish successfully. Reasons vary. The person going through may make choices that result in failed resolution, and their spouse may choose a road away from the one in crisis. There is no right or wrong way of navigating the swift-running waters of the midlife crisis. However, the possibilities that can occur because of the crisis are many, containing various combinations. A few of the known possibilities and alternate roads the person in crisis can take are listed below.

First Possibility
The most desirable outcome exists within the realm of successfully finishing all aspects within the midlife crisis. Once out of the final healing process, life takes on a settled appearance, and the person in crisis experiences the return to a normal existence. However, due to the crisis that has permanently altered their outlook in a positive way, no traces of their experience remain.

Because of the steps taken during their crisis and healing stages, they have strengthened their moral code, corrected former faults, and reached emotional maturation. In addition, they are stronger, capable and more resolute. Their relationships no longer define them, as they are now capable of defining themselves. If a spouse exists, they have chosen to remain married.

These are the true successes, and this is the result you wish for your midlife spouse, as they walk into a successful future within all aspects of life.

Second Possibility

The midlife spouse is too emotionally weak to face their various issues and continues to avoid facing Self. As a result, their crisis is put on hold, and they become stuck in an emotional rut of their own making. However, it is only a matter of time before the crisis returns as the issues within resurrect and, once more, overwhelm the person in crisis.

Until they gain the strength to overcome the emotional weakness and move forward, they remain in this state, enduring recurring bouts of crisis. This causes deep concern for their spouse, because there is no way to help someone who does not want nor will accept help. This often results in the left-behind spouse deciding they have had enough, and chooses to move on, with a divorce looming on the horizon.

It is extremely difficult to deal in this way, because the midlife crisis offers no guarantee of resolution. The choices are clear--move forward or remain stuck. Through time, perseverance, patience, love, and the God's strength, one can become most able to deal with the situation. Only God knows what lies ahead within an uncertain future. Therefore, it would behoove the loving spouse to look to God for clear direction and instructions on what to do, if anything, to help break the recurring cycle.

<u>Third Possibility</u>
The midlife spouse is deeply engaged within an illicit affair and chooses to divorce their loving spouse. Their altered thought process wrongly dictates that their pain will be resolved by legally ending their marriage. To add insult to injury, they choose to marry their mistake.

These midlife spouses have chosen to begin and maintain a continuing affair. Because they choose not to see any other way out of their ongoing troubles, they take the path of least resistance, choosing to leave an old life behind to start a new one. Regardless of the reasons for their decision, they do not realize or care that this mistake will follow them the rest of their lives. Biblical wisdom speaks of one reaping what they sow, and consequences, though lasting a season, will be compounded many times over upon one who chooses this road. One will endure the results of their chosen path.

Because they initially cheated with the mistake they chose to marry, it is possible that their mistake will do the same to them, or they will become restless and cheat again with another.

The midlife spouse becomes stuck in a seemingly endless loop of consequential events, true happiness is denied them and the affair partner who has cast their lot with the one who continues in crisis. It is still possible to resolve their crisis if they choose to put forth the effort into choosing the correct path. However, if they choose to remain stuck within the rut of their current mistake, resolution may lie in sight, but remain just out of reach for life.

<u>Fourth Possibility</u>
A midlife spouse can choose to disappear without communicating with their wife or husband for a long period, lasting up to seven years, or longer. When ready to return, they show up on their spouse's doorstep. If allowed to return, they may speak of the experience or decline to answer questions. However, after some time, close observation reveals they move forward into the last stages of the midlife crisis and go on to finish the healing experience. Very little data exists in this area with only one case validated.

The other possibility that exists within this twofold aspect is the midlife spouse who returns only to find the left-behind spouse has remarried during the time of their disappearance. This raises the question of which person the left-behind spouse will choose. If they choose the one, they have married because of circumstances, this will usually result in the midlife spouse going through the exact same emotional upset they once caused their left-behind spouse to endure when disappearing without notice.

Final Possibility
Once the midlife spouse has vacated the household, the abandoned spouse may undergo a radical change of heart. Understandably, they may feel the marriage is over, and think their midlife spouse is permanently done with them. This is the sole choice of the left-behind spouse, because the midlife spouse chose to gamble everything on the presumption they could return whenever they chose. The possibility remains that the left-behind spouse may turn their back on the midlife spouse, thus preventing their return.

Divorce becomes an option and if there are any feelings left within the midlife spouse, they go through the same emotional upset they caused their spouse when they left home.

Summary
In each of the above possibilities, the midlife spouse emotionally abandoned their left-behind spouse long before the physical abandonment occurred. Even though physical abandonment does not always occur, it remains a distinct possibility within the midlife crisis.

Regardless of the reason or justification behind each of the undesirable possibilities, there is never an excuse for willful actions designed to destroy a marriage and family. One must consider the consequences carefully before deciding any action. Unfortunately, the midlife spouse does not stop to consider their destructive actions because their state of mind is totally focused on Self, often to their detriment.

A gentle reminder: Never forget, nor discount the power of God within your life and marriage. There is hope as long as love remains.

Chapter 5

The first step of the journey takes courage, and requires a deep Self-examination,
which involves overcoming the fear of discovering that you are just as human, therefore capable of making mistakes, as anyone else.

This topic is a major aspect of the midlife crisis. These children of their issues tend to show up in stage three of the crisis, Total Emotional Regression, lose emotional control, and cause a lot of damage. Before moving into a deeper study of stage three, one needs to gain a greater understanding of these children, their role, and resolution during the midlife crisis.

<u>Who are these "Children"</u>

Midlife crisis is a time for growth and healing of emotional, spiritual and mental aspects never faced in childhood, complicated by the physical battle involving their past issues. These come in the form of the "children" who were damaged long ago, made up of the broken pieces within their psyche.

Various psychological journals explain how the children are present throughout a given person's life, not just during the marriage. These speak of the inner child and ways to care for them, but not many journals speak of how to fully resolve them. The children pop up from time to time, long before the midlife transition, in response to disagreements or emotional buttons triggered. These same children are also part of the coping mechanisms one uses to deal with various troubles within life.

These are an unhealthy part that need facing, resolving and healing. When these inner children come out and are not resolved, they are placed on the back burner for later. When a major life change comes, the inner children come out to deal with it, and situations are dealt with using the tools that exist within these same children. But they don't recognize or understand how to resolve issues until the midlife crisis comes about and forces the issues to be resolved to bring the imbalance into proper balance.

The chemical and hormonal changes at midlife are the catalyst for the beginning of the biggest trial one will face. This trial includes the rising of <u>all</u> the children of the issues. In the past, there were single children that came up from time to time; that single child could be pushed back down. During the crisis, <u>all</u> the children rise, band together, and attack. They cannot be ignored or pushed back, as it is time to face Self and grow up.

The Child versus the Core Personality

The child (or children) takes the driver's seat of the one in crisis. The core personality is also present, standing with and alongside the child, but the core personality has no control over the child's actions. The core personality can influence the child, but not make the child do anything it doesn't want to do.

The child also shares some memories with the core personality, but the child does not have to accept what the core personality holds in the way of memories. The child can rebel heavily against what the core personality tries to communicate. The core personality is often ignored and very often disregarded while the child does whatever it wants.

The child acts from the emotional memory of what happened to them before their emotional piece was hidden within the shadows of the psyche. The puzzling thing for the child is the fact that there is no one from their past, and the left-behind spouse is a total stranger to them. It is not the core personality that sets the marriage aside; it is the child. Why? The child was not married at the time of the abuse or hurt, and it certainly is not married when it surfaces. That is why the left-behind spouse is seen as controlling, authoritative, and manipulative to the child who is determined to do as it pleases, regardless of who it hurts.

Note: To keep the children from destroying the core personality, the feelings of the one in midlife crisis are buried to protect them for a later time.

THE PROCESS OF RESOLUTION DURING THE CRISIS

The Past Issues of the Midlife Spouse

From the time of birth, all humans are meant to undergo proper physical, emotional and mental training to achieve full maturity by the onset of adulthood. However, due to a parent's past emotional history, a child is usually reared to adulthood based on what their parents know at the stage of their own growth and based on what these same parents learned when they were children. There are other factors involved, including various generational mistakes, but each contribution (right or wrong), is geared toward raising children to be just like their parents.

To be fair, parenting does not come with a one-size-fits-all instruction manual. People do the best they can with the knowledge they have. Each child comes equipped with its own personality, and the handling of each one is often vastly different.

Parenting is a true challenge, because the goal should be to raise children who are balanced in all ways. However, the most common imbalance, during the formative years, is the emotional aspect. Many people's childhood years were a repetitive cycle of torment that led to a destruction of their self-esteem, self-worth, and self-confidence. Instead of being understanding, parents often unintentionally emotionally abused their children.

Their attempts to raise strong children by telling them to "grow a thicker skin", or "stop being so sensitive", only led to greater feelings of alienation and deeper feelings of not being enough. Other issues involved feelings of inadequacy, going unnoticed, or jealousy of a child whose siblings received more attention. They probably felt they were more trouble than they were worth but were not able to communicate the feeling out of fear no one was listening. Coupled with one or both parents facing a midlife crisis during the child's formative or teenage years, there were many emotional obstacles to overcome.

Sadly, many people endure the final rebellion[1] of puberty without resolving any issues carried over from their childhood. However, in time, these same issues return to be faced again, whether in young adulthood, or during the transitional period of midlife.

The Children of their Issues

These children represent each negative experience that happened during childhood. At the time of each occurrence, an emotional piece was broken off and placed within the shadow of the psyche, to be accessed when the time would be right to resolve it. Due to factors such as their inability to cope with what was happening and their mental and emotional immaturity, the child subconsciously suppressed damaging events, internalizing the resulting blame, guilt and shame.

---

[1] The rebellion is simply the major sign of emotional immaturity within each person who does not choose to accept they have been thrust into the threshold of 'Change, Growth and Becoming'. This is primarily emotional, but also spiritual, as these two aspects are neglected by most people because logic tends to override both aspects. In logic, people are not confronted with their shortcomings in either emotional or spiritual areas.

Whether it was divorce, abandonment, emotional, physical, mental abuse or a combination of these things, the fact is there was a major life changing event that caused more pain than the child could bear. As the child struggled, they internalized the negative things, and built an emotionally insulated wall against further hurt. They also developed a self-victimized attitude to cover up their inability to control their environment. The child couldn't risk handling it on their own, because deep inside they knew it would shatter them into emotional and mental pieces. This is a survival tactic for self-protection.

The mind can shake life-shattering events, detach and shift them into the emotional realm where all the pain is felt. Logic can't feel hurt, but emotion can. The resulting emotional distance becomes a buffer, an emotional cushion, against the causing of more damage. There was an immense amount of emotional and mental damage done by that life-changing event. Because the child cannot shoulder any more damage, they distance themselves from both the act and the person that turned the emotional wheel in a negative direction.

Children do not (and are not expected to) have the proper mental and emotional skills to understand or resolve an issue that appears as a result of being on the receiving end of devastating damage. Therefore, the issue created is then put on hold for a later time.

Another opportunity to resolve these childhood issues comes during puberty. However, if there is no one available to help them work through the issues, they will again be buried within the shadow of the psyche for a later time. If there has been past damage within a person, these will present as multiple emotional pieces throughout the midlife crisis.

It's been said that the Quarter Life transition occurs at age 25 and brings another attempt to resolve issues, because the brain finished maturation around that age. Failing that, another opportunity comes forth at the time of midlife.[1]

Emotional History Repeats

Very few people reach the middle of life bearing the ability to cope with the future. Everyone is forced to turn back, because the journey into the past must be navigated, faced, resolved and healed in full before that person can even hope to continue forward into deeper emotional growth.

As a person passes through the first two phases of the midlife crisis, the loss experienced during this early time, whether perceived or real, triggers their desperate attempt to maintain control of their environment.

However, in preparation for the third stage, Total Emotional Regression, the midlife spouse is emotionally stripped[2], exposing their bare emotional bones. When the protective cover of logic is removed or suppressed, the emotional side is strengthened. They are left defenseless, unable to cope and deal as they once did. Since their personal defense mechanisms no longer work, they challenge everything they were taught earlier. As a result, their perception

---
[1] Life scripts are fully discussed in the chapter, "Midlife Defined."
[2] Or going through complete disintegration.

skews as their entire life becomes a series of questions, accompanied by feelings that something is missing.

These questions represent "The Children of the Midlifer's Issues", who are preparing for their own internal onslaught upon the unsuspecting person in crisis. The children from their unresolved issues emerge and start showing.

As emotional regression continues, the one in crisis experiences increased feelings never felt before, due to heightened emotional awareness. During this time, their prior logical thinking, which has always governed their lives, is set aside in favor of emotional thinking and reasoning. They begin experiencing a deep confusion that leads to the onset of intense anger. This heavy anger is likely to lash out at anyone without warning. It is the child that throws the emotional bomb upon the left-behind spouse.

<u>Emotional Scattering and Regathering</u>

When the emotional door to the third stage opens and the threshold is crossed, all hidden emotional pieces within the psyche are scattered to the emotional wind. It is up to the one in crisis to locate these emotional pieces. This triggers the aspect of emotional cycling. This moving back and forth tends to help the spouse in crisis gather different emotional pieces as they continue the process of slowly putting Self back together.

Each emotional piece fit into place contributes to future growth. It is not unusual to see them come forward positively for a period, then move backward in a negative fashion. No person can move forward positively without moving backward negatively. Without movement of this kind, they risk getting stuck in an emotional rut of their own making. They need to go backward to process what has happened to them, just as they moved forward within a given aspect. This same cycling is also seen when the spouse in crisis moves in close for a time, then moves away for a time. This is called a touch-then-go[1]. For a greater understanding, see the Chapter entitled, Emotional Cycling.

Each person within midlife crisis will have more than one time of regressing, or emotionally going backward. However, going backward (or rewinding) in an emotional way, is necessary to come forward (progressing) in a stronger way. This is a much-needed part of their growth, change and becoming[2], since there is much to outgrow within the emotional aspect of their personal lives.

This aspect of emotional cycling continues throughout the midlife crisis until all pieces are gathered, (faced, resolved, healed), and finally, fit into the space reserved for each one.

The Appearance and Behavior of the Children

Since the children are also various fragmented pieces within their main issues, they are broken down further into manageable parts

---

[1] A child or a teenager will also, "touch then go," during the time of pubescent growth.
[2] Growth, Change and Becoming is the purpose for the midlife transition / crisis. To grow, change and become all that God intends one to be.

and pieces. The person in crisis will face each child as they have the strength and the inclination to resolve that issue.

The children of their issues will appear off and on during the midlife crisis, making their appearances irregularly. These do not always stay in residence[1]. If they stayed in residence constantly, the person in crisis could not function. One never knows when one of the children will appear. These children <u>do not</u> appear in order of chronological age. For example, one time a young child may appear; the next time, a teenager; and the next time, a child aged between the two.

While a child is in residence, the person in crisis is unable to learn new things, has trouble with the simplest of jobs, and is more likely to ask for help, even if it seems they will not take the help offered. Some of these same children sound like broken records, repeatedly bringing up the same things. They seek validation for their feelings, as they are truly victims of their not-so-recent past. Since the midlife spouse has unresolved issues from childhood that come forth in the form of certain-aged children, one will see an even greater immaturity than before, as their inner child comes forth seeking healing.

It is important to recognize the despair and deep depression seen within them. Compassion and empathy should be shown toward the midlife spouse while, at the same time, guarding self-respect.

---

[1] This statement is contrary to the belief of some others.

Resolving the Children

Once each child is resolved, another piece is fitted into its proper place, and the child in question is not seen again. However, as long as there are issues remaining within the person in crisis, various children will continue to come forth. What and how issues are faced depends on the midlife spouse. This aspect of facing their various issues is as individual and unique to each person as the crisis is.

These children also tend to appear as the opposite of their personality when their emotional damage was done. Apparently, the original behavior they exhibited did not work the first time around, so while they work their way through the second childhood or second puberty, they often go to the opposite side of the spectrum to try what wasn't tried the first time. This opposite behavior usually shows in deep rebellion. Some of the children, especially the incredibly young ones, show more hurt than anger.

The older children and teenagers more likely show deep anger, and even rage at the wrong(s) done to them. They act out in the form of tantrums and angry outbursts that do not make sense unless one knows the history of the midlife spouse.

There are many things a midlife spouse may spew at the left-behind spouse in relation to their childhood. At times, it may seem as if the spouse was the one who hurt or damaged the midlife spouse. These times come as the midlife spouse exhibits the behavior of one who views their spouse as a stranger, because the child would not have known the spouse at the time of harm. These are the times when the midlife spouse is reliving a time before meeting their spouse.

<u>Recognizing the Children</u>

When the childlike behaviors appear, pay attention to the eyes, as these are the windows to the soul.

When exceedingly small children come forward, they have a wide-eyed innocence. When viewing older children, the wide-eyed innocence is mixed with the rebellion of one at that age, daring something be done about their behavior. A teenager shows the harder look of one in either near or complete rebellion, and may tell the left-behind spouse, "My life is none of your business". Within their perception and through the eyes of the midlife spouse, everyone is expendable and when the child gets bored, they take steps to discard the old and find a better fit for the child's need of unconditional love.

Speech and behavior are usually dead giveaways in guessing the age, especially to those who are parents. The phases of development are not hard to recognize when their actions bring forth memories and aspects of the development years of one's own children.

A midlife spouse's time of reliving their past is akin to emotional time travel, only it takes place within the mind. It is during these revisited childhood or pubescent times there will be no recognition in their eyes for you. To explain, you will be seen and spoken to or regarded as a total stranger. At this state, their mental life is within a time before you were known by the person in crisis. The human mind is a complicated organ subject to various chemical changes; anti-depressants would help, but since the person in crisis does not want help, they will not get nor take medication.

Also, in this time of revisiting early childhood, the one in crisis is not capable of providing care or emotional support because they are in a time of redevelopment. Most spouses in midlife cannot be trusted with the care of young children. This is simply because they are not much more than children themselves during this mental and emotional time.

Wisdom for the Left-behind Spouse

Many people become upset when they observe their midlife spouse emotionally cycling. They feel as if they are constantly caught off guard and walking on eggshells with a spouse nice one minute, angry the next. This is clear evidence that the children are in play and struggling for emotional control within the midlife spouse. Time, patience, love, understanding, and a willingness to stand aside is needed. This provides the emotional space the midlife spouse needs to do what they feel is necessary for Self.

During this time, their lives are shattered, and they must learn to put themselves back together as best they can. As a gentle reminder, the midlife spouse is on their own timetable. They will do what they feel they need to do, when they need to do it. Nothing can be done to influence them one way or the other. The left-behind spouse has two options: Continue to stand for the spouse in crisis or walk away.

Here are words of advice to help you navigate through this time of crisis:

- Facing the children of their issues is a spiritual aspect of the crisis and the resolution must be done within. God alone can help them.
- Do not ask the midlife spouse for anything that represents responsibility. This adds pressure to them. Rather, work on being friendly but distant.
- Let the midlife spouse come to you. If you go to them, it is considered pursuit.
- Do not allow compassion for their emotional pain to get in the way of what you must do to protect yourself and take care of your children.
- A person in crisis cannot be disciplined as you would a wayward child. Therefore, allow them to fall. Reaping and facing their own consequences is the only way to learn their lessons. Just as a child learns from their mistakes, so must the person in crisis.
- Trust the Lord for all that comes. Allow your intuition to guide you. The children will continue showing until every past aspect of damage is faced, resolved, and healed within the midlife spouse.
- Remember, you have no control over what your midlife spouse does. You only control yourself, your actions. reactions and responses. Let go of your midlife spouse and allow God to do His necessary work within their life.
- Set firm and loving behavioral boundaries to protect yourself and retain self-respect. Once a behavioral boundary is set, hold your ground within this area. (More information in the chapter on Boundaries.)

- Stand strong and pray for endurance. The 'crazy' person you see is not your spouse but one of the children of their issues acting out. It is the child who creates the chaos. It will be the core personality who shows remorse, makes permanent changes, and leads to the better person, in due time.

Chapter 6

Temptation leads into a harsh test of character.

The Peak of the Midlife Crisis

Stage three, Emotional Regression, is the longest stage of the midlife crisis. Much damage is done to both spouses during the complete breakdown of the midlife spouse. This section covers aspects, behaviors, and the midlife affair that occur during this stage and are touched upon in this chapter.

Events, behaviors and avoidance tactics occurring during this part of the crisis include, but are not limited to:

- Total Emotional Regression
- Controlling Behaviors
- Running Behaviors
- Escape and Avoid Tactics
- Opposite Behaviors
- The Midlife Affair

Total Emotional Regression occurs when an emotional door opens leading into the past, exposing unresolved issues during earlier development. Once the first issue is targeted, whether it is faced or deflected, the midlife spouse finds Self at another undesired emotional place. Stepping across into the opposite side is necessary to begin an important emotional battle with the evil side[1] of one's Self.

---
[1] Often called the "shadow side".

During this time, controlling behaviors[1] become predominant, such as justification, arrogance, projection, angry spewing and confusion. In addition, running behaviors[2] come into play such as wearing the mask, the midlife affair, vanishing, and escape tactics.

The midlife spouse feels unworthy as the battle against the evil side of Self waxes hot. Keenly felt, every negative emotion comes forth for examination. Coupled with their already painful issues, this aspect becomes too much to bear. Pressure builds inward that spews outward.

The emotional attachment, with a person outside the marriage (if formed) becomes stronger, leading them toward inevitable temptation. Their hearts and minds turn from their spouse.

Guilt and shame change into fear which transforms into white hot anger. In time, all these things spew outward against the loving spouse, who has some idea that something is wrong but does not know what is about to happen. The core personality[3] knows they are wrong but cannot do anything about it. To protect the feelings that remain, these are buried beneath layers of justification used to send the midlife spouse's marriage to its death. When emotional pressure reaches critical mass, the inner child[4] that has control of the midlife spouse drops the emotional bomb.

---

[1] See Chapter, "Controlling Behaviors" for more information.
[2] See Chapter, "Running Behaviors" for more information.
[3] The core personality does retain full awareness during the crisis.
[4] These inner children are explained in great detail in the chapter, "The Children of their Issues".

Left-behind Spouse Forced into their own Journey

As was predetermined by this life's process, it is now time for the left-behind spouse to join the midlife spouse in a journey that is connected, yet, at the same time, separated. This blindside is a necessary event that forces the left-behind spouse onto a road they neither wanted nor created.

The process itself dictates this aspect, because there is no other way for this to happen. Conventional wisdom says no human would willingly subject themselves to such emotional pain without being forced into it. The result of this pain is the same for all spouses drawn into its depths. In time, Change, Growth and Becoming what God meant for both people begins. The bitter cup has been forcibly handed to the left-behind spouse, and the die has been cast. The spouse who has been abandoned, (at least for this time) begins a time of emotional struggle as they try to figure out what happened.

Little do they know, a major midlife crisis is in process, and their marriage has been thoroughly disposed of by the person they thought they knew. Life as they once knew it has ended, and within these various endings, a new beginning lies ahead. However, the path ahead is unclear, and a deep grief clouds the eyes of the left-behind spouse, who has loved faithfully, truthfully, and blindly.

If the left-behind spouse looks back, they realize things were not quite right in the near distant past. However, each change came so subtly, it was difficult to put one's finger on the cause, as there seemed so many. Other signs in hindsight are the infrequent bouts of anger, tantrums, threats of leaving for no apparent reason, moodiness, cranky behavior, crying spells, and the left-behind spouse feeling the need to walk on eggshells.

No spouse ever wakes one moment and decides to wreck their

marriage in the next, it is simply impossible. A decision of this kind is never made suddenly. To say the beginning of the crisis started at the emotional bomb drop is to discount the various signs seen long before this occurred. Not every marriage was a bad relationship. Although there are some marriages filled with varying degrees of unrest and serious problems, one could not say this about every marriage.

The midlife spouse from the past was a stable, responsible person who took their marital role seriously. The left-behind spouse never imagined their gentle loving spouse would become a spitting, snarling animal, constantly blaming them for everything. But because the midlife spouse cannot face Self, they turned completely against the left-behind spouse. This did not happen overnight but was a gradual slide into these depths which began with the aspects mentioned above.

Once the complete emotional break has occurred, the midlife spouse moves ahead into the next phase, while continuing to leave their spouse behind to find their way through this maze of uncertainty[1].

Midlife Crisis | Crossroads

The Crossroad of Temptation for the midlife spouse leads one of two ways, as it causes their strength of character to be thoroughly tested, leading into a Stand or Fall. To 'Stand without Falling' means God directly assists the midlife spouse. To 'Fall without Standing', means God only does what is necessary to help the

---

[1] An entire section has been devoted to the left behind spouse, to explain life's lessons, the journey forward, and how both the journey of the midlife spouse and the left behind spouse coincide. Be encouraged. God stands with the "Stander".

midlife spouse move forward[1]. Few people make it past this time without 'Falling' into sin.

Whether a Stand or Fall is accomplished, wandering in the wilderness becomes deeper, because the midlife spouse continues their quest for self-identity. As the emotional battle continues to rage out of control, increased struggling between the light and dark side continues.

Emotional cycling occurs as they swing back and forth from one behavioral extreme to the other. The emotional pendulum swings wildly during this time causing deep mood swings. Restless feelings mixed with irritability and times of irrational anger are followed by remorse, confusion, depression, and withdrawal.

The left-behind spouse becomes confused because the midlife spouse is constantly up and down from one day to the next. Dealing with these extreme mood swings can become nerve-racking because one never knows which mood they will be dealing with.

The extreme emotional pendulum swings become worse as the midlife spouse tries desperately to hold on to the negatively repeating emotional cycles. These cycles are comprised of outside solutions to fix inside problems meant to make them feel better about Self. Most often described as self-medicating or running behaviors, these will include, but are not limited to:

---

[1] It is not that God is unforgiving. Forgiveness for a Fall can be asked for and given by God, but not without consequence. One of those consequences is the loss of God's direct help. Woe is the person who allows themselves to Fall! God would rather they make a Stand that is firm and faithful, steadfast and true. His heart grieves heavily for the one who has Fallen

- Alcohol and drugs
- Large sums of money spent
- Full abdication of responsibility
- Continued avoidance and projection behaviors
- Midlife affair
- Various sexual addictions, such as pornography, dating sites, sexting, cybersex, and sexually explicit exchanges with people outside their marriage
- Acting out the definition of true emotional insanity which means trying the same things repeatedly, attempting to reach a different result

Dead End Roads

Life eventually becomes redundant, boring, and repetitive, closely resembling what the midlife spouse thought they left-behind. The dead-end roads that looked so inviting become exhausting, as it becomes more trouble than it is worth to keep up consistent appearances. Various masks[1] begin slipping, because past issues are subconsciously settled within, resulting in change to growth. The midlife spouse grows restless once more as they become dimly aware of disturbing realizations that begin tugging at the edge of their subconscious mind.

Their carefully crafted fantasy world shatters, as they find they can no longer maintain their former highs. The boundaries set against their undesirable behaviors by their left-behind spouses begin to take their toll as each escape route is firmly closed against reentry. As a result, the consequences for their wrong behaviors overtake

---

[1] More about the wearing of masks in Chapter "Running Behaviors".

them. In addition, they discover their affair partner is not what they thought. In addition, if alcohol, drugs, or sexual addictions are present, these become empty, and are no longer the kind of fix they once seemed to be.

The money that financed their former way of life runs low. In desperation, they sell things to maintain this façade. However, nothing lasts forever and the affair partner (who mostly wanted the midlife spouse for their deceptively endless funds), either seeks to abandon them for another or pressures them for what they can no longer give. The midlife spouse is again trapped in an emotional cycle they created. A definite and marked increase in confusion appears, which brings about fear, then anger, because things did not turn out as planned. Their expectations crash, triggering a deeper confusion, fear and anger.

The First Awakening | Awakening to Self

As this portion of the emotional crisis goes into the next phase, reality shines the Light of Truth into the situation. This is not a good showing, because this triggers self-victimization that leads into emotionally distancing behaviors from the acts the midlife spouse has perpetrated. There is no one left to blame except Self. They know this but cannot admit it. If they were forced to confront Self before being mentally and emotionally strong enough, it would drive the midlife spouse into a complete nervous breakdown. If a mental and emotional breakdown happens, there is a possibility they may not return from that state, and if they did recover, they would never be the same.

The midlife spouse is in a fragile state, caused by their inability to reconcile the evil person who chose this path of destruction with the good person who would never do such things. They view these two people as the same person. As difficult as it is to understand, this emotional distancing from their actions is a self-protective move on their part[1]. Despite the emotional pressure they endure, they intuitively know they must protect their currently weak state of mind and emotion, by using strong self-victimization. The commission of suicide becomes a greater possibility during this time because pressure equals desperation and greater emotional pain.

Due to this extremely weak state of mind, they insist what has happened is the fault of everyone else. According to them, things have happened to them, not because of them. They prefer to shift responsibility elsewhere instead of taking direct responsibility. Their actions to trigger events which caused great damage to Self, spouse, and family is projected upon others, and deflected. This shows failure to own their wrong actions. Because of their present childlike state of mind, they suffer from the ability to reconcile Self with their wrong actions.

However, despite this and other behaviors, they are forced into the Awakening to Self. They understand if they do not do damage control, all will be lost. The midlife affair (if present) will be ongoing, the midlife spouse will still be emotionally broken, but their hold on their delusional state of mind is slipping.

At this point of awakening, the first third of the recent damage will be revealed, and a hole will appear in the midlife spouse's high-energy balloon. As this balloon continues to leak, they lose altitude. Although every effort is made to pump this high-energy balloon back to its former state of height, this loss overruns and overtakes them, sending them into the next aspect of this emotional journey.

The downhill slide toward the fourth stage begins. Emotional

---
[1] As discussed in the Chapter "Children of their Issues".

struggle intensifies during this time because of fear and uncertainty about the unknown future. Emotional and mental clarity continues to increase within the midlife spouse. A concentrated effort is made to connect with the left-behind spouse because fear of loss has also been triggered. The gradual slide downhill toward the facing of their failures becomes sharper and pronounced. The crossover that leads into the fourth stage begins to come into view, as does the emotional tightrope[1], designed for the left-behind spouse to walk.

Observations of the Left-behind Spouse

From the point of the awakening of the midlife spouse, the left-behind spouse should see a positive change of attitude, an emotional turning back, as their once buried feelings resurrect. There should also be a softening.

Flashes of the old, flashes of the new, and flashes of the person they will become at the end of their journey will be seen. In addition, the childlike clothes worn during the earlier part of this stage should gradually change back into the style worn before the crisis.

The midlife spouse will show signs of wanting to become emotionally close to the left-behind spouse, hoping to do damage control as they realize they are facing possible loss of the relationship. To prevent this, they try to bring things back together. This is a time of new discovery, and the left-behind spouse is advised to show love, acceptance, and an open heart, allowing the midlife spouse time to build a new connection. This is a time of dating, coming back together, and getting to know one another.

Bear in mind, the midlife spouse is on a quest to find their lifetime

---

[1] More about the emotional tightrope in Section 4.

companion. The left-behind spouse wants to be that choice and should allow history, children, past marriage and their marital stand to speak for itself. Dare to hope the midlife spouse will realize their left-behind spouse is the best choice.

The personal attitude of the left-behind spouse is especially important during this time. Begin setting loving and strong behavioral boundaries on the midlife spouse. As long as the midlife spouse continues rebellious behaviors, they are not ready to navigate out of this stage.

If the midlife spouse comes to the awakening, it is an emotional turning point putting them on a downhill slide toward the journey into the next stage, Facing Total Failure. This next stage is the lowest point of the midlife spouse's journey. The extreme emotional experience they undergo during this time begins the journey into the latter half of the midlife crisis. The emotional road becomes increasingly difficult for both people. This is the toughest leg of their journey, because the highs they used for emotional survival begin to gradually recede. As a result, the increasing depression takes them into the emotional lows that must occur for emotional change to continue taking place within Self.

Serious emotional instability should show, because they clearly do not want to approach the point of crossover leading into the fourth stage. Something in the midlife spouse knows this crossing will lead steadily downward into a very low place of depression, called rock bottom. This is similar to a time when a teenager navigating through puberty experiences deepening depression to the point, they, too, hit rock bottom, and perceive that the only way out is up.

However, the midlife spouse's journey downward is a much longer stretch than puberty's aspect. For an adult in midlife, there is more emotional damage to face than there would be for the teenager struggling during puberty. Though the midlife spouse and the teen going through puberty know the difference between right and wrong, teenagers are not much more than children still learning, and have only damaged themselves. The midlife spouse is an adult who has accumulated enough life experience to directly recognize the severe damage they have done to their families and Self.

However, midlife spouses will seek to distance from the collateral damage they have committed during this time, because their emotional health is still weak and malleable, much like the teenager. Until enough strength is gathered to enable them to face and confront Self, they continue to avoid what they have done.

Patience, love, and understanding by the left-behind spouse will serve best during this time. It is strictly up to the left-behind spouse whether the midlife spouse's overtures are accepted or rejected. Remember, the midlife spouse is still too emotionally weak at this point in the journey to bear the whole burden of accountability for the recent damage perpetrated against all aspects within their lives. Full accountability should come forth during the fifth stage. It is advisable that, for now, the once-broken emotional connection be allowed to rebuild. This would hopefully lead to an emotional re-bonding that should sustain the couple through the last three stages of the midlife crisis.

The next chapters provide deeper explanations of the behaviors and aspects of the midlife spouse mentioned above.

Chapter 7

Having respect for someone is about giving them space and the right to make a choice for themselves, even if you don't agree with what they are either about to do or are doing. Right or wrong, they are adults, therefore accountable for their real and perceived mistakes. All you can do is step back, set firm boundaries, let go, and let God work His will within a given situation.

This section gives an idea of what to expect in the way of behaviors and aspects, but there are many others not included. As each person is different, each midlife crisis is different. Differences show based on each person's unique way of navigating this time of emotional trial.

Like the hallmarks, enough aspects are seen within the crisis to identify what is happening. Many of these behaviors and aspects are seen throughout the crisis, especially during stages one through four.

Controlling Behaviors of the Midlife Crisis

The midlife spouse fears losing control of relationships and situations. What they do not realize is, though they think they are the controller, they are controlled by their need to control. This is a terrible emotional prison created by the midlife spouse, who is unaware the prison is of their own making. They are trapped in anger, misery, and depression, yet the key to freedom, called Change, Growth, and Becoming, is hanging beside the door. All they need to do is reach for the key, but in the midlife crisis, there will be much damage and running before the key is taken and used to bring freedom.

In this chapter, various controlling behaviors used by the midlife spouse are explained, as well as survival skills for the emotional wellbeing of the left-behind spouse. These are listed in alphabetical order, as shown below:

- Anger, Spewing and Confusion
- Blame Shifting
- Chaos
- Confusion
- Control and Manipulation
- Deflection
- Defensiveness
- Double Standard
- Drama
- Projection

Anger and Spewing

The nearly constant anger begins in stage two and reaches its zenith during stage three. Anger intensifies as the midlife spouse realizes no matter what they do, nothing changes within the realm of time.

They are angry and irritable at everything and nothing calms them. It is similar to what happens in pubescent teens as they struggle to become adults, and that rite of passage is difficult at best.

Intense bouts of anger within the midlife spouse can be triggered through various situations they do not handle well. Inward pressure due to past issues continues to build, eventually causing them to spew. They appear to be on emotional edge most of the time. The lack of emotional control combines with inward-to-outward rebellion. As a result, one sees more anger spewed in various ways; even to the point of turning inward, as in the case of depression. The midlife spouse is aware of their anger but cannot seem to help themselves because they are emotionally out of control.

The anger spewed is based on several things:

- Their past issues and the people in their past who caused these same issues.
- Their real and perceived failures within Self. (Being miserable becomes anger at Self.)
- The feelings of being stuck. These are compounded by the guilt, shame, misery, and pain they feel. They hurt, but since they do not want to look within, they lash out.
- Guilt and shame become fear, which translates into anger.
- The constant internal pressure from the emotional, mental, and spiritual battles within bring out their dark side, triggering angry spewing.

The midlife spouse uses anger to intimidate anyone who tries to hold them accountable for their actions. It is also used in disrespectful ways toward people who put pressure on or emotionally push them. The setting of boundaries against them makes them angry, and they project their anger upon the left-behind spouse every chance they get.

Angry accusations speak to their growing dissatisfaction with life. They create arguments to give them justification for their rebellious behavior. Anger clouds their judgment, and decisions are made that often lead to serious destruction. Blame and justification are used to ensure they do not have to take responsibility for the destructive results that happen as their anger spirals out of control.

No one likes to see this kind of anger; however, it does serve a purpose. Quite often, anger brings clarity when nothing else works. In addition, the midlife spouse's anger can serve to cut through their deep confusion and help shine a temporary light into their muddled thinking. On the other hand, this intense anger can also bring forth actions that are eventually regretted.

Not every midlife spouse shows constant anger. However, they all have serious struggles within that lead to times of intense anger. Though constant anger may not be directly witnessed by the left-behind spouse, this does not mean their midlife spouse has not experienced, or will not experience, this aspect. As they continue processing within the facing, resolving, and healing of their past issues, these bouts of constant anger eventually resolve in full.[1]

---

[1] Ongoing bouts of anger can be seen as late as the final stage of the crisis. However, these bouts show in a different way, as the midlife spouse continues emotionally cycling, at times open to vocalize how they feel, other times closing down to process within. The midlife spouse becomes completely aware of their anger at that point, making more of an effort to get it under control as they continue growing. They are sincerer in their apologies for their show of anger. The guilt and shame over all they have done in the way of damage continues to fuel their anger until it burns off completely.

Blame Shifting

Blame shifting tactics are used because the midlife spouse cannot see Self as being at fault nor take ownership of their wrongs. Shifting blame is used to project their feelings onto the left-behind spouse to attempt to influence them to take responsibility for the breakdown of the marriage. Within their skewed thinking, who best to continue baiting into taking the blame for what is clearly the midlife spouse's internal problems?

Chaos

The left-behind spouse didn't damage their spouse all those years ago and was not present when the damage occurred. But because the left-behind spouse has issues of their own, they take on the midlife spouse's problems and carry a burden of shame, blame and guilt that doesn't belong to them. The midlife spouse skips off until eventually returning for their projection fix.

The cycle begins again as the left-behind spouse fusses, argues, and tries to put everything back the way it was. The midlife spouse blames, shames, guilts and off-loads their bad feelings onto the left-behind spouse. Because the left-behind spouse doesn't understand that nothing they do or say will make a difference in the crisis of their spouse, they participate once again in the negative cycle.

The reason these cycles repeat is because the one who lives in chaos does not know how-to live-in peace. Chaos gives them attention, just like small children who create drama. Chaos does have a purpose because order eventually comes. Until order is found, built or created from a balance, chaos will continue to reign. Such as the crisis that is being faced.

Confusion

Before the crisis, the midlife spouse coped with their emotions by covering them with logical thinking. In midlife, their logical thinking is suppressed, forcing them to learn to deal with their feelings. The key to coping in this new way is hidden within their emotional past, but they do everything possible to avoid finding this key.

Because their emotional thinking is weak, unused and unexercised, their decisions are made through confusion. For example, confusion is evidenced at the time of the unwanted emotional bomb, when the midlife spouse informs their husband/wife, "I love you, but I'm not in love with you".

When the left-behind spouse exerts pressure on the midlife spouse to understand what is happening, the direct result from the midlife spouse is often angry spewing, arrogant justification and deep confusion. This behavior is designed to force their husband/wife to back off.

The more upset the husband/wife becomes, the more justified the midlife spouse feels in their hateful words and actions. They say things like, "If you didn't get so upset, I wouldn't do what I'm doing or say what I'm saying." Or perhaps, "If you wouldn't do or say this, I would do or say that." Another example, "If you'd just leave me alone, I wouldn't do or say these things." It doesn't matter that what they are doing or saying is wrong.

After the anger calms down, deep confusion sets in. Why? Because somewhere within the midlife spouse's core personality, they know they were wrong in the way they acted or spoke, yet they don't understand why or how they reacted as they did.

Control and Manipulation

Controllers and manipulators are dependent on someone else to control and manipulate. Why? Because one cannot control and manipulate in a vacuum. They need someone to provide the fertile ground, so they have "other control", which is the control of other people. They can't control Self, so they seek to control others, which gives them someone to blame for their immature actions. All emotionally immature people are controllers, manipulators, and require outside validation. The midlife crisis did not create this problem, it just complicates it.

The midlife spouse is driven to control and manipulate their environment and everyone in it, especially their left-behind spouse. They do this for at least two reasons. First, they perceive their left-behind spouse is as bad as they are, due to the codependent factor within the midlife spouse who has not separated Self from their spouse. Second, they turn the definition of insanity in an opposite direction. The definition of insanity is doing the same thing over and over, expecting different results. The typical midlife spouse creates change for everyone within their reach without expecting anything to change for them. They do this to prevent change from happening to and against them.

When things go their way, everything is okay. When a situation shifts, and change causes them to suffer or lose control over something or someone, they are spurred to action.

One of the biggest mistakes a left-behind spouse makes is in allowing their midlife spouse to continuously control them. Based on the fear of losing their midlife spouse, they continue to give information to the same midlife spouse that decided they did not want to grow up, be married, or responsible. Yet the left-behind spouse works to stay connected rather than detaching and releasing the emotional rope. This lack of separation leads to the midlife spouse constantly blaming, shaming, and projecting their negative feelings upon the left-behind spouse.

When the midlife spouse wants something, they shift emotional sides to keep the left-behind spouse confused. When they don't get what they want, the niceness disappears, and emotional war begins again on the side of the midlife spouse who is out of emotional control.

The midlife spouse twists the left-behind spouse's goodwill by confusing them, using guilt, and blaming the left-behind spouse on their actions and behaviors[1]. These behaviors are classic manipulator moves and mind games.

---

[1] For example, the midlife spouse may say, "If you didn't act in this way, I wouldn't respond as I do."

The midlife spouse has their own best interest at heart. If accused of wrongdoing, they respond by name-calling, or they spew, argue, justify, then blame the accuser. They are masters of the twisted word and action. Most say if the left-behind spouse were nicer, they would not do what they do. That's not true because it's pure projection on the part of the midlife spouse. However, if the left-behind spouse does what they say, they find a way to twist it and take advantage of the left-behind spouse. If one makes a stand against them, they twist that as well.

Midlife spouses use angry outbursts, tantrums and other behaviors to trigger fear in the left-behind spouse. They do this to gain control of a situation and manipulate it for their own benefit. This is a major issue they didn't overcome in childhood, so the inner child returns to see if what didn't work then will work now. Immature people don't like being told no nor shown they have lost "other" control. They must learn they do not control anyone without their emotional permission.

Defensiveness

The midlife spouse fears their left-behind spouse will try to stop them from doing what they want to do. This fear leads them to defensiveness. Even if the left-behind spouse tried to stop them, they would find another way to accomplish what they want.

Deflection

A midlife spouse will often confess to one thing to prevent confessing to another thing they are unable to face. In addition, they try to use someone's love against them, as when one loves they can also be hurt. Love, to a midlife spouse, is perceived as a weakness that can be used and exploited; their perception about love is used to their (dis)advantage.

Double Standard

Midlife spouses tend to live out a moral and ethical double standard defined as "one set of rules for me (midlife spouse), and another set of rules for you (left-behind spouse)," or "I can do everything while you can do nothing." It seems okay for the midlife spouse to rebel, destroy their marriage, family, and life, but if the left-behind spouse follows suit and does those same things, the midlife spouse judges them harshly.

It's part of "Look what you did – that was wrong! But don't you dare look at me! You have no right to judge me for what I've done, because I'm justified, and everything is your fault!" Midlife spouses can point moral and ethical fingers at others but do not want the same finger pointed at them. In their view, they're above the rules that regulate behavior. If they feel the left-behind spouse is out of line, the midlife spouse erupts in anger and a confrontation often ensues. There is a certain level of perfection set by the midlife spouse that involves no allowance for mistakes made by their left-behind spouse.

One example is in spending. The midlife spouse decides they are entitled to all the money, but if the left-behind spouse spends money, regardless of the purpose, the midlife spouse becomes angry and tries to control the spending of funds. Somewhere within, they know this excessive spending on their part isn't a good thing, but in their entitlement and lack of self-control, they do it anyway.

Another example is when the midlife spouse commits adultery against their marriage. However, when the left-behind spouse follows suit, the midlife spouse is unforgiving. This is where the same double standard comes into play. Midlife spouses want to be forgiven for what they have done but if the left-behind spouse does the same, it is not acceptable.

To hold the left-behind spouse to a higher standard simply goes back to the fact the midlife spouse gives Self emotional permission to morally rebel against what is right while withholding emotional permission for their left-behind spouse to do the same. Bottom line, it's a controlling behavior on the part of the midlife spouse because they seek everything their way while dispensing judgment upon the left-behind spouse for every mistake made.

The left-behind spouse often doesn't understand they are being observed by the midlife spouse. The farther the left-behind spouse rises above the situation, takes the high road and lives out that higher standard of moral and ethical behavior, the worse the midlife spouse's behavior becomes.

The outward behavior of the midlife spouse speaks to not thinking very highly of the left-behind spouse, but their inner knowing dictates that the midlife spouse is not worthy of someone as good as the left-behind spouse. They may do everything possible to try and chase the left-behind spouse away from them, but that's because they feel they really don't deserve good things, or even the love of a good spouse. The midlife spouse knows the truth, but distances from that truth.

They know what they are doing when they are doing it, they know it is wrong, but they are driven to do it anyway. It's a constant inner war between knowing what's right and doing what's wrong. It's like they set aside the cost that is going to be extracted for their sin and make the situation worse.

Drama

The midlife spouse creates drama for a variety of reasons, including:

1. Feeding their justification for their actions.
2. Gaining and maintaining control.
3. Avoiding accountability.
4. Attempting to flip their bad-person complex back onto the left-behind spouse.
5. Justifying their actions[1].

The most confusing part of the drama is no matter what the left-behind spouse does, the midlife spouse sets them up to be wrong,

---

[1] This is very similar to a teenager in puberty who is emotionally unsettled within and seeks to cause chaos in every situation they encounter. The troubled teen also overreacts (at least in a parent's estimation) to any setting of limits or boundaries.

while the midlife spouse is always right. Some left-behind spouses seem to continually walk on eggshells, not knowing what will trigger these bouts of drama. Again, this is one of the many controlling aspects of the crisis.

Another goal of creating drama is to see how far the midlife spouse can go before seeing their bad-person complex neatly flipped back onto the left-behind spouse. If the situation goes too far, the left-behind spouse can lose control, saying and doing things that cannot be taken back, and whatever is said will be filed away within the memory bank of the midlife spouse to be brought back as ammunition for another time. In this way, they continue playing on the guilt of the left-behind spouse for having lost control.

Projection

The midlife spouse hates and cannot accept Self. They maintain the inability to face what they feel and lack the emotional strength to view Self honestly. Since they look to outside sources to validate, justify and make Self feel better, they project onto their spouse. This is done in the hope they will never have to see the issues for and within Self. It is easier to project what one feels onto someone else than to turn it inward for an honest facing.

Projection is when the midlife spouse blames, shames, accuses, shifts responsibility and accountability, and tries to manipulate their left-behind spouse into taking on what they do not own. This is due to past codependent tendencies between the two and is a connection that neither person can break for a period, in spite of the fact the midlife spouse has already distanced emotionally and often physically. This codependency, in the past, led to the automatic taking of responsibility for their partner's feelings. It is through this connection the midlife spouse feels justified in projecting upon their spouse. The left-behind spouse believes the negative feelings, wants, needs, and blame for things they do not own.

Because of this inability to separate, the midlife spouse assumes they know how their spouse feels and what they have done, yet the spewed accusations don't match the true feelings or actions of their spouse. This aspect makes projection confusing, as the left-behind spouse struggles to make sense of what was said.

Projection can also be a type of emotional rewriting used to cover what the midlife spouse knows is unacceptable behavior, both past and present. The midlife spouse separates the bad from the good, keeps the good, and emotionally distances from the bad. Most of the time, they are unaware of trying to project an undesirable behavioral quality onto someone else to avoid facing it.

For example, most midlife spouses accuse their spouse of criticizing when they should not. However, it is not their spouse who criticizes, but the midlife spouse who has this tendency or problem. At first, this accusation confuses the spouse, until the realization hits that the midlife spouse is being hurtful. In making this accusation, the midlife spouse justifies their behavior because they do not have a valid excuse for their actions. The midlife spouse is projecting their feelings of being too critical onto the object of their also projected self-hatred, their left-behind spouse.

As long as they are allowed to project bad feelings and behaviors onto their spouse, they continue avoiding Self by forcing their left-behind spouse to carry the responsibility and blame for their various shortcomings and mistakes.

Projection runs its course, and given time, the spewing and confusion will end, and the midlife spouse will have to face Self anyway.

Response of the Left-behind Spouse to Controlling Behaviors

- The left-behind spouse did not break the midlife spouse; therefore, the left-behind spouse cannot fix the midlife spouse. This is their journey.
- The midlife spouse is living in a past time before they knew the left-behind spouse, and though it seems their anger and behaviors are directed at the left-behind spouse, this is not always the case. During times of anger and spewing, get out of the way until they cool down.
- Detach[1], emotionally distance, and stay calm, even though simmering under the surface. Allow the midlife spouse to express and resolve anger they were unable to unleash during their childhood. This is a necessary part of navigating the midlife crisis. There are two things a midlife spouse cannot argue with: a closed mouth and a person who is peacefully entrenched in total detachment.
- Set firm and loving boundaries[2] to prevent the midlife spouse from control and manipulation. They may become angry and reject the boundary, but their conscience will

---

[1] More information on Detachment in Chapter, "LBS Healing Process."
[2] More information on Boundaries in Chapter, "Life Lessons."

engage them in battle to work through and overcome their anger. No matter what is said or done, the anger within them must come out to eventually burn out.
- Do not feed their drama or other controlling behaviors. Refuse to engage. Back off, leave the room, walk away from any nonproductive discussion. They are looking for something to keep the blame deflected from Self. Release the midlife spouse to their own devices, ways and choices.
- Understand it is good for the midlife spouse to spew, as this often brings clarity, brings their anger to the forefront, and releases some of the pressure.
- Watch and listen. All actions and words of a typical midlife spouse are confused and make no sense but are often laced in truth. The words often speak to where they are in crisis, and they often reveal things they are unaware they are saying.
- The cycle of allowing control and manipulation must be broken by the left-behind spouse. This break triggers emotional unrest that must be used to set boundaries to protect Self. Stand firmly to deal with the emotional storm that will follow. Being forewarned is always forearmed because the controller and manipulator will seek the deny the change of situation that will eventually teach them, they aren't always going to get what they want.
- It is a waste of time to try and stop anything the midlife spouse sets their mind to. They will do what they want to do when they want to do it.
- If one can step back and compare the behavior of the midlife spouse with a pubescent teen, they will understand how the midlife crisis works and better see the similarities between the two.

- Do not validate any projection behavior when there is not truth in it. Simply look at them and wait. If one set of projections do not work, they will try another to convince the left-behind spouse to take responsibility for a deep emotional problem that belongs to them.
- Controlling behaviors are common and are not to be taken personally. The midlife spouse is in search of Self and tries to avoid everything using these behaviors.
- Look beyond the bad behavior to see the hurting person and learn to separate the behavior from the person. Bad behavior is only a symptom of extremely painful emotional issues within that hurting person.
- Learn to simply listen and say nothing, regardless of what is said, and these behaviors will lose their effect.
- Understanding these behaviors are part of their avoidance behavior will go a long way toward gaining strength to endure this stage.
- The left-behind spouse has no control over whether the midlife spouse owns their actions, behaviors or words. It is best to focus on Self and the healing of Self.

Encouragement

Hurting people tend to hurt people. Eventually the smoke and mirrors used by the midlife spouse to deflect attention from Self clears, and they will see reality. Once they move toward the honest facing of Self, the usage of these behaviors will not occur as often and eventually stop. The midlife spouse will find their own healing from within, and no one on the outside can fix them.

Chapter 8

*The midlife crisis is not about the marriage, nor the marital foundation,
nor any relationship that existed before this trial. The issues started long before then.*

One of the hardest aspects to explain about the midlife crisis is the emotional pain experienced within the midlife spouse. It is a deeply ripping, rendering and tearing pain, coupled with voices that torment the midlife spouse, both day and night. There is no escape.

As explained within the beginning of the third stage, there is a certain emotional door that opens bringing the midlife spouse face-to-face with their issues of the past. Their skewed perception often leads them to believe there are monsters in the dark. Though they will do things like leave the television or lights on, nothing keeps their terror at bay.

Each piece of the past has a voice of its own, competing with the next to gain the attention of the midlife spouse. Out of fear, the midlife spouse tries unsuccessfully to shut them out. Failing to do so pushes the midlife spouse to extremes to be free from these unwelcome mental and emotional visitors as well as the emotional pain. The typical midlife spouse lacks the understanding that gaining inner peace means directly facing, resolving, and healing these past issues. Because this facing is so terrifying, they often choose to use running behaviors and tactics to avoid this facing of Self, including but not limited to the following:

- Abandonment
- Alcohol and Drugs
- Emotional Cycling*
- Emotional Splitting
- Escape and Avoid Tactics
- Midlife Affair*
- Opposite Behaviors
- Spending
- Vanishing
- Wearing the Mask

*Note: Emotional cycling and the midlife affair are discussed in succeeding chapters.

Abandonment

The person suffering with abandonment issues is so frightened of being left-behind they emotionally and sometimes physically abandon someone they love before the one they love can abandon them. To keep from having that direct experience, they set up circumstances that leads them to doing it first before their greatest fear happens to them.

This is an avoidance tactic used to keep the fear at bay as well as keeping others at arm's length. These people have suffered abandonment events in childhood where their parents abandoned them emotionally and/or physically. They internalize these aspects and feel something was wrong with them, not the one who abandoned them.

Because of this perceived unworthiness developed over time, they often go through one failed relationship after another searching for what they cannot find: perfection. They ascribe to the thinking that life is a fairy tale, and no problems should occur. When things go wrong, they are frightened of being abandoned by their spouse.

They are unfamiliar and uncomfortable with what a settled life looks like. They were conditioned to live as a survivor in chaos. They are unsettled within Self and subconsciously seek to recreate familiar circumstances. They don't understand being accepted because they cannot accept themselves. They are puzzled when they act out and are not asked to leave. Their expectations are such they are defective; therefore, no one could love them or want them around. Because they have never figured out the problem is within Self, they project their personal abandonment feelings onto the one they love the most, usually their spouse.

They are driven by internal emotional forces beyond their control. They have never been taught to finish what they start, never been taught what true love entails, and they have no idea what commitment means.

Response of the Left-behind Spouse to Abandonment

- It requires strength, patience and love to stand firmly and not be swayed by what is seen in outward appearance. Only God knows what goes on within the heart and mind of a person who suffers abandonment issues. All one can do is

pray for their spouse, set the boundaries necessary against bad behavior, and let God do the necessary work within the midlife spouse to help and heal their longstanding emotional wounds.
- The spouse with this issue needs constant reassurance. On the other hand, their behavior is contradictory and confusing. They are, at times, clinging and demanding. Other times, they are emotionally distant and closed. Because they lack communication skills and the recognition of knowing where these feelings of abandonment come from, they cannot possibly vocalize their pain.
- Until the person who suffers from abandonment issues reaches a point of facing, resolving, overcoming and healing these issues, they will continue to repeat the same patterns experienced in childhood.

Alcohol and Drugs

The running behavior of using alcohol and drugs is an attempt to numb the pain they feel. Though a common running behavior, not all midlife spouses use drugs and alcohol to dull their inner emotional pain. Others abuse only alcohol, others only drugs, and even others heavily drink and use drugs. The dangers of both aspects are varied, with a chance of addiction to either or both.

Large amounts of alcohol and/or drugs can cause aggressive behavior on the part of the midlife spouse, causing trouble and/or physical fights while drunk or high. It is better to leave well enough alone, and pray the midlife spouse breaks these habits on their own. If their actions result in an arrest of any kind, do not interfere or bail them out.

Response of the Left-behind Spouse to Alcohol and Drugs

- Intervention is a consideration in helping them past an addiction, however, one must be careful if this choice is made within the realm of extreme circumstances. Everything the left-behind spouse does is suspect in the eyes of the midlife spouse, who does not want help. All actions, however well-intentioned, are often seen as controlling on the part of the midlife spouse and can result in their running farther away.
- If faced with trouble, the midlife spouse must also face the resulting consequences. If the left-behind spouse covers for the alcoholic, and/or drug addict, this is enabling behavior. The left-behind spouse should set an appropriate boundary and distance from the situation as much as possible, so the midlife spouse has a proper incentive to stop the behavior on their own. Draw the line firmly, step back, and watch the midlife spouse learn to deal with the consequences of their own actions. Be prepared to intervene only in a matter of life or death. In time, this aspect should pass.

Emotional Splitting

The midlife spouse is aware of the wrong done to Self and others when they fall into temptation, though they do not understand why they chose to do wrong. During the time of Total Emotional Regression, they distance from that "other person" who fell.

Emotional splitting is where the "person" who committed the wrong is divided against the "person" who would not have fallen in such a way. This is not called compartmentalizing, because the "good person" is aware of the "bad person". Their words reveal they are aware of what they have done, but since they cannot accept their bad behavior, they push it away or distance from it.

Even if shown undeniable physical evidence of their wrongdoing, they deny committing such a wrong. This self-protective response is because the midlife spouse does not have the emotional strength to fully reconcile the good and bad.

Response of the Left-behind Spouse to Emotional Splitting

- Even those not in crisis fail to reconcile their opposite sides, as they seek to repress and deny the dark side. To achieve a solid emotional balance within Self, each person must accept the fact that light and dark sides are contained within everyone. True human nature consists of maintaining a balance within.

Escape and Avoid Tactics

Escapism and avoidance are not exclusive to the midlife crisis. These self-serving coping mechanisms are used for the first half of an immature person's life to push away or ignore responsibility and manipulate others into carrying their burden. These tactics helped the immature person cope with adult issues they could not handle. As long as someone else reaped in their place, they successfully escaped and avoided consequences for their childish actions.

But in time, a major life's event occurs, and the irresponsible and immature person is called upon to face everything previously escaped and avoided. Unfortunately, there is no escaping or avoiding a certain accountability required to call the midlife spouse into a time of Self-reflection. If escapism and avoidance could be used, the midlife spouse would not be in an emotional crisis. They would successfully escape and avoid the facing of all issues. But that's not possible because all real and perceived escape routes to bypass or avoid this time of change, growth, and becoming, are closed. This loss of previous coping mechanisms triggers panic as well as a desire to run away from everything they once knew and loved.

Response of the Left-behind Spouse to Escape and Avoid Tactics

- Let go of any responsibility or burden carried for someone else. Set a boundary and do not take on the responsibility of another person. The one the boundary is set against will fight to prevent carrying their own responsibility. Stand firm and enforce the boundary.
- Carrying the responsibility of someone else enables them to escape the consequences and will prevent them from growing up and carrying their own burden.

Opposite Behaviors

When the midlife spouse dropped the emotional bomb, in their mind, they ended the marriage and crossed into the world of opposites, which brings forth Full Emotional Regression. This exploration of the opposite side of Self is mandatory and no one is immune to this time of growth intended to strike a balance between the good and bad sides of people. (See Emotional Splitting above)

- What they once loved is now hated.
- They were married, but in their mind, became single.
- Where they were attached, they are now detached.
- They were a mature adult but are now an immature child.
- They were once moral but are now facing the temptation to become immoral.
- Where they were predictable, they become unpredictable.
- What you think they will do, based on what you once knew, they will not do.
- What you once thought they would not do, they now do.
- Where they were once logical, they are now emotional.
- Where they once walked in the light, they now walk in the dark.
- Where they once acted in character, everything they do becomes out of character.
- In the spiritual aspect, where they once believed in God, they now question God.
- Their successes now become failures.
- Their failures now become successes.
- Their perception of you, which was once loving, now becomes deep hatred.
- Their trusting nature becomes paranoia.
- Their gentle nature becomes violent.
- If they played it safe, they now take risks.
- Where they were good, they are now bad. The bad is immature behavior that must be outgrown and matured.
- Their emotional needs that were once met by you, now go unmet, because you're no longer an emotional "fit" for them.
- Their feelings for you, once strong, no longer exist, as those feelings are unconsciously buried under layers of wrong justifications, and they are forcibly detached from these.

- They become different. They become the opposite of the spouse you once knew, trusted and depended on.

The next step of this journey takes them into a crossover that sends them from the light side they lived and loved, to a dark side they fear, hate, and struggle to overcome. The battle is painful, deep, and intense as their past issues are released from the Shadow of the Psyche. These released aspects overrun the midlife spouse, and the voices of those painful issues rise in desperation, seeking vindication, justice, and eventually peace.

It takes courage to come forth and risk rejection, but the painful issues of the past will not be denied. When it is time for these issues to begin the process of maturation, they know they must have the cooperation of the core personality which acts as a gate keeper. The core personality will regulate the flow of the self-centered, miserable, damaged and immature issues so each one has it's time in the spotlight within the stage that involves Full Emotional Regression.

Once vindication is complete and full restoration is finished, the past issues are forced to return to the psyche, but no longer as prisoners of the shadow side of Self. All wrongs have been made right and healing will commence.

<u>Response of the Left-behind Spouse to Opposite Behaviors</u>

- Where there was once respect, disrespect takes over and is a major contributing aspect of immature thinking and actions. It's also the foundation of childish and teenage behavior. Set a boundary against disrespect that sets limits on

what you will and will not tolerate in the way of behaviors that directly affect you. Disrespect says they will lie by commission and omission, thereby depriving the left-behind spouse of information needed to make fully informed decisions. Disrespect calls names, controls, manipulates and threatens. Disrespect steps outside of marriage, gets into another relationship before resolving the current one. Disrespect blames, shames, guilts and projects.
- Be patient and quiet. The midlife spouse is doing the best they can, and it will take time to figure out why they did what they have done. They must work this out and reconcile their good and bad Self in full.
- At the First Awakening, there will be a gradual return to the person you once knew, but it will take time, as they still must reconcile Self and the marriage in full.

Spending

Because the midlife spouse is deeply entrenched within a teenage mentality, they may waste funds the left-behind spouse needs to support their families.

Response of the Left-behind Spouse to Spending

- Protect the resources and finances needed for household, children and Self. The midlife spouse is not going to be responsible, so the left-behind spouse needs to formulate a plan and stick with it. Especially if there is another person involved. It is important to set a firm boundary in the financial area.

Vanishing

Midlife spouses are filled with fear of being controlled and manipulated by the left-behind spouse trying to fix them by emotionally smothering them. Some run, some hide, and some vanish. Some walk away for good, some return. Whether they stay or go usually depends on the emotional stability of the left-behind spouse. If the left-behind spouse refuses to walk their own journey, they become miserable, constantly depressed, and deeply absorbed in their own hurt.

The more immature both spouses are, the more likely the midlife spouse may vanish completely. Why?

Because the left-behind spouse is obsessed with their midlife spouse, emotionally smothering them, while refusing to step back, let go, and walk their own journey. This attitude is without regard or respect that everyone has a right to an adequate amount of space to change and grow. To continue being exposed to the left-behind spouse could be emotionally detrimental to the midlife spouse, based on their state of mind. Until their state of mind changes, the midlife spouse will not reach out to the left-behind spouse, and that is if they ever do. Not all left-behind spouses behave this way, however, in each case of vanishing seen, there was a left-behind spouse wanting to control and manipulate their midlife spouse.

The midlife spouse cannot take emotional pressure and will run from it. The more pressure, the farther they run. They are in a war within Self, struggling to emotionally survive, regardless of their actions. However, even if a midlife spouse vanishes, they keep tabs on their left-behind spouse and always know where things stand.

Response of the Left-behind Spouse to Vanishing

- Do not act like a parent to the midlife spouse and do not try to force behavioral changes.
- Let go of control and manipulation; this will only drive the midlife spouse further away.
- Break the mindset that dictates what is best for the midlife spouse. This is too much for them to handle.
- It is perfectly acceptable to reach out to the vanisher and test the waters from time to time. It is also acceptable to pray for them and ask God to continue to work within their hearts, praying, "Thy will be done."
- God has the big picture and full knowledge of what the future brings. Obey His direction or instruction, that often comes through intuition.

Wearing the Mask

The Mask is used by the rebellious midlife spouse to hide inadequacies within Self, whether real or perceived. This includes the children of their issues, which they perceive would not be well received. They use the Mask to hide from the world, without the concern of being completely exposed to those who know them well. This is similar to what an abuser does. They show the world the "good" person, but in private, the "good" person mask drops, revealing the "bad" side of Self to those who know them well.

There are two different masks a midlife spouse uses to hide or shield Self during the crisis. One is a mask worn in public that comes off in private. The second is the mask worn to project a certain image to their affair partner. This section covers the public versus private mask. The mask worn with the affair partner will be covered in Section 3.

Public Versus Private Mask[1]

This mask is worn to keep people from seeing who they really are. In public they are nice to others and the left-behind spouse. In private, the mask comes off and the left-behind spouse sees the abusive midlife spouse. Why? The midlife spouse cannot allow those outside the immediate family to see them as they are in crisis, so they project what they want others to see.

The midlife spouse feels their left-behind spouse, who knows them, will allow them to act any way they choose. Therefore, the left-behind spouse always sees beyond the mask. It's a form of crazymaking on the part of the midlife spouse, because people on the outside have a hard time understanding that the one in crisis acts one way in public and another way in private. Eventually, the mask slips under pressure and the midlife spouse are seen as they are at home.

---

[1] There is also a second mask, "The Affair Partner Mask" that is described in, The Midlife Affair).

For what it's worth, the people at their workplace, especially their boss, are usually among the first to see this aspect, knowing something is wrong, but unsure what to do. If the behavior of the midlife spouse becomes bad enough, they may lose their job, become dissatisfied, or quit.

Response of the Left-behind Spouse to Wearing the Mask

As long as the mask is worn and the façade is maintained, they feel there is no reason for change. Yet at some point, the light of reality will shine the light of truth into the heart, their eyes are opened, and a crossroad will be faced. Everything done during the crisis to avoid the facing of Self will prove to be a waste of time, because:

- For each day the midlife spouse refuses to buckle down and focus on their inner-Self, they are getting that much older.
- For each day the midlife spouse chooses to seek outside solutions to fix inside problems, the left-behind spouse is moving that much further away from them.
- For each day the midlife spouse continues engaging in running behaviors designed to avoid their inner issues, they are hurting Self that much more.
- While the situation of the midlife spouse becomes worse, the left-behind spouse has the opportunity to make their situation better by leaning into the journey toward wholeness and healing.

Chapter 9

The truth is, you must face the past before you can face the future. In the past lies the key to your future growth. If you're not willing to look backward, it becomes difficult to look forward. What isn't faced within yourself will always return to torment you. You can run from it, hide from it, bury it, but it doesn't work because it always returns to be faced – it's only a matter of time before it does. That's a major portion of a person's journey that leads toward wholeness and healing.

As long as the midlife spouse continues dealing with the issues alive and "unwell" within, they will move back and forth (emotional cycling) from good to bad behavior. These mixed messages can be confusing, as one day they are a best friend, and the next day they are the worst enemy, with the latter showing more often than the former.

<u>Teen vs. Midlife Similarities</u>

Midlife crisis is an emotional developmental process, much like teenagers trying to find Self. It should not be surprising that the issues faced by the midlife spouse are much like the teen who struggles in some of the same areas. Both use drama for control and manipulation to gain and keep control of various situations. Both stop at nothing to get their way including throwing tantrums, acting openly hostile and being difficult to live with. Their attitudes are filled with anger, self-pity, self-victimization, and self-hatred. Both are crying out for boundaries, although they announce they do not need help. The differences are as follows:

- The teen has their life ahead of them, whereas the midlife spouse has reached midlife, with a job, spouse, children, and bank account.
- The mental capacity and maturation of both parties. The teen doesn't have the necessary mental tools to resolve their issues without help. Because of this, their issues are buried within for a later time. The midlife person has the mental capacity and maturation to face their issues, as life has taught them some things. But upon reaching midlife, they are aware there is something wrong that bears examining. Because of the fear that swells within, they choose to run instead of taking the more difficult path of facing, resolving and healing Self in full. They do their best to drown out and avoid the issues to keep everything on a superficial level.

Although the midlife spouse is completely rebellious, and as unbelievable as it sounds, they want to make sure their left-behind spouse will still be there. Though they may try to convince Self that life would be best apart from the left-behind spouse, their unbroken connection continues to bring them back.

<u>Response of Left-behind Spouse to Behavioral Cycling</u>

To break the cycle calls for a change in behavior, reacting in a way the midlife spouse does not expect. The left-behind spouse must overcome fear, release worry about the outcome, refuse to be the recipient of bad behavior, and stand against what is wrong. This is not to punish the midlife spouse, but to protect the left-behind spouse from the behavioral cycling. One can't lose what has already been lost in the fires of the midlife crisis. After all, if the midlife spouse wants to leave, they will leave.

Rather than being a doormat, the left-behind spouse must be resolute, strong, and intolerable of wrong behavior. When a course of action is set, let go of expectations of how the midlife spouse will react. The decision of what will be tolerated and taking steps to change the situation, through actions or a confrontation, is the equivalent of saying "no more" and not backing down. The actions taken will depend upon the situation.

For example, the midlife spouse seeks to control the left-behind spouse with anger and threats when confronted with things they do not want to discuss. They do this by saying hurtful things to shut down the conversation. Upon recognition of this cycle, it can be stopped by changing behavior and reactions to hurtful statements.

In this same example, the midlife spouse threatens to leave or remove something by using emotional blackmail or attempting to control and manipulate the situation. The response is to ask the midlife spouse to either leave or carry out their threat. The left-behind spouse should not go back into the behavior of crying, pleading or begging, which encourages the behavioral cycle. Standing up to the threat breaks the cycle.

Piecing Things Together

No issues are seen or evaluated by the midlife spouse until they are ready to move from the second stage, *Loss of Emotional Control*, into the third stage, *Total Emotional Regression*.

Since the midlife spouse contains all their emotional strength at that point, the first issue seen will be the most difficult and painful to face. It is fear that drives them to run from Self for a period. It is no wonder they use various running behaviors such as drinking, drugs, and even the midlife affair escape this necessary first facing.

The midlife affair, although primarily used to avoid facing Self, can be the main vehicle used to work out parental issues, as the affair partner can be just like the midlife spouse's parent or parents. Though hard to understand, if one knows the midlife spouse's past, one may be able to follow along as the midlife spouses progresses through this aspect of the midlife crisis. This issue can be worked out in its entirety, or it can be worked out in various pieces, just like piecing together a jigsaw puzzle. Before entering the issues of each problem, they were missing various pieces within Self even before the crisis drew them into its tight grasp.

During this time, the whole of their personalities undergoes a further disintegration, reducing the person to an emotional shadow of their former self. This disintegration process triggers a process of reintegration, rebuilding, re-piecing within each person. This has many aspects for completing Self, given time.

It is seen where the pieces must go to rebuild or re-piece Self, but the person going through is the only one who can locate each piece within. The new or missing pieces will appear as the process continues. These should be picked up and pieced together, as they are ready to begin and continue the necessary work on Self. Once the picture is complete within, they become whole and healed with every piece in place.

Before this completion happens, however, there are many pieces, or aspects, that make up the whole of each issue. It is not uncommon to work out one part, put it on hold for a period of time, then return once ready to work out the next pieces, or aspects, of the puzzle or issue for Self.

For example, it's not unusual to work out part of an issue in one stage, and attempt to move forward into the next stage or two to keep moving steadily forward. But when an attempt is made to progress forward before issues are resolved, they may have to return to an issue faced partially within a former stage. If they do not return, they can become and stay stuck within the stage they are in until they do what is needed to move – whether forward or backward.

Cycling backward may be necessary to locate missing pieces to the main issue they are facing, as well as the necessary aspects surrounding each issue. Cycling backward is done to continue forward and complete the work needed on and within the issues.

This piecing is not only for resolution of each issue and aspect, but also sets up the emotional cycling of the midlife spouse. Incomplete issues within a given stage are the reason doors to various stages are left open for future accessibility. Some doors are simply cracked, while others are left wide open.

It often appears the midlife spouse goes through one or more stages at the same time or skips certain stages. They are not allowed to skip any of the stages. They may piece together various elements at one point, move forward to piece other aspects, then move back to piece more, as the various pieces are found or become available. They can do whatever they choose when they choose. It is their puzzle to piece together. They can put various elements and aspects on hold for a time, then return to work on more of the aspects of their numerous issues. Watching them can be confusing as they cycle back, forth, and through to catch aspects they missed beforehand, due to incomplete facing, resolving and healing on their part.

As they move between various stages, whether forward or backward, they gather more pieces to work into their puzzle. As each puzzle piece goes into place, the picture continues to form within Self. What is not completed will stay open until the issues within are complete; right along with the supporting pieces, or aspects of each one. The cycling will not complete until they have completed processing within, and all issues from the past stages have been faced, settled, and healed.

Puzzle Piece Analogy

Using the analogy of a jigsaw puzzle will help examine and explain the possible ways a midlife spouse can work out their issues. This also explains why they are prone to emotional cycling.

For example, one empties a thousand-piece puzzle onto a table with the intention of piecing it together. One starts by piecing together the outside border of the puzzle. This frames the puzzle and sets the stage for a more accurate piecing to eventually attain the whole picture.

The main elements within a puzzle would be pieced next. For example, the guide picture might show a house, a barn, a pump house, some trees and a lake. Of course, no puzzle of this type is complete without grass to enhance the look and feel of the completed puzzle. Time is spent piecing the various main elements together. If certain pieces for one element can't be located, another element can be pieced together as the pieces are available for each one. In time, all pieces for each element are found and pieced in place. This helps contribute to the eventual completion of the entire picture.

Time is also spent looking back and forth for missing pieces needed to complete each aspect. There is no right or wrong way to piece together a jigsaw puzzle. How it's done or not done is totally up to the one working it. If one so chooses, they can walk away for a period, only to resume the work when it's convenient. Eventually all the main elements come together. Once these are done, the smaller details, such as the grass pieces, are brought together, one piece at a time, to complete the task. Once every piece is in place, the puzzle is complete. Applying this analogy to the journey of the midlife spouse will hopefully give more understanding of this necessary process.

In the life of the midlife spouse, this time of change follows a process of tearing everything down. This may look unhealthy because of the internal battle that has worked its way outward. But remember, the midlife spouse does this to Self because they rebel against everything, they know is right, and they are the only one who can control this. They are fighting between right and wrong, good and evil, and will either win or lose the battle. The internal battle does external damage for as long as the person fighting said battle continues to engage. For that reason, their mental and emotional health suffers, as well as their countenance and physical appearance.

The Need for Space

The emotional pain within the midlife spouse completely consumes them and their heart and thoughts have turned against the left-behind spouse during this time. They have nothing to give and have no room for needy people. It is like a cornered animal whose need is survival and comes out fighting.

The left-behind spouse is advised to accept and emotionally adjust to this change, detach, and distance from the drama, putting the focus and energy on Self. It is respectful to back off and give the midlife spouse what they want and need, which is the emotional space to learn how to deal with Self. The midlife spouse will demand space loud and clear in many ways by saying things such as:

- "Leave me alone."
- "Back off."
- "I can't do this."
- "I will smother to death if I don't get away."
- "If you don't stop, I will leave."
- "If you don't shut up, I will get a divorce."

- "I can't stand this anymore."

These statements are midlife crisis script, but the midlife spouse has feelings, wants and needs. During this season, total detachment, emotional distancing, no contact, and going dark are emotional tools used to benefit the left-behind spouse[1]. These emotional tools help the left-behind spouse rebuild their strength, regain their balance and do necessary self-healing. These tools are not games to control and manipulate another person. They are designed for the left-behind spouse to use for their own benefit.

Any influence that once existed with the midlife spouse is no longer there. Their view of the left-behind spouse is skewed, perception is twisted, their perspective is off, and this is beyond the control of anyone except the midlife spouse. Respect and grant their need for solitude.

When the source of emotional pressure is removed, the midlife spouse often begins closing the emotional gap. The release of emotional pressure triggers their insecurities, fear of abandonment, fear of loss, and fear that the left-behind spouse will move beyond them, never to return. True, the midlife spouse has rejected the left-behind spouse, but once space has been created through the respect of solitude, separation anxiety often occurs. Some people will not choose to turn back until they perceive the emotional door is closing on them. Others run for that door when it has closed to the point of almost locking them out.

---

[1] Further explanations of these emotional tools are found in the chapter titled LBS Healing Process.

Remember, feelings cannot be switched off quickly. Though the feelings the midlife spouse once had are buried under layers of justification for their wrong behavior, deep within they do not want to lose their spouse. They need space to learn to deal with Self, so they are not allowed to use their left-behind spouse as an avoidance tactic.

The Purpose of Cycling | Emotional Rebuilding of Self

In midlife, every person who has not achieved emotional maturity will be broken down and their former foundation, built on emotional wounds caused by emotional damage of one's past, will be deconstructed and rebuilt into an emotionally mature adult. In this taking apart process, all emotions are deconstructed into as many emotional pieces as necessary to reconstruct those pieces into a new Self. Pieces that will not work for the future are discarded as Self is rebuilt. In this rebuilding lies emotional maturity.

Good and bad comes together to be sorted out; the good is set aside while the bad is endured, withstood, and overcome. The final resolution in the process leads to transforming the bad into the good, as the major life lessons are learned. Now, within this developmental process, the midlife spouse struggles to outgrow the emotionally immature aspects they have always contained within.

Once someone is made aware of the issues they need to face, resolve and heal, those issues do not go away. They continue to return to poke, prod, and push one into action. If one refuses to learn the various lessons and resolve their issues in midlife, the various lessons cycle back. Each cycle becomes harder to endure, and the time of trial becomes longer. The more one struggles against this necessary learning, the more miserable they become. It is something to consider.

Satan is active during this time of trial and will do whatever is necessary to keep the midlife spouse stuck in ongoing sin that results in soul-rending guilt, shame, and – if he can succeed in keeping them down – they will continue to lose touch with their sense of Self.

And it all takes time. Time to make an emotional adjustment and time to readjust to the unwanted change that has been thrust into the lives of both spouses. This journey does change the perception and perspective of the midlife spouse. As their personal direction becomes clearer, they discover who they are, solidify their self-identity, and make changes to bring forth a balanced individual. Using the right materials, they rebuild Self into a better person, learning to relate, think and speak differently and maturely.

From Repression to Resolution

There are four steps within this scripted action to move from repression to resolution:

- *Regression.* Going back to the time where and when the issue occurred.

- *Resurrection.* The issue is brought forth from its repressed state, and the emotions are relived as if they happened the day before.
- *Recognition.* It is part of the growth process to recognize what happened was not okay.
- *Resolution.* To resolve an issue, one must accept, forgive and heal from what happened. Then one must achieve the change and growth of becoming a more mature adult.

The above process repeats for each unresolved issue. Once resolved, one learns the life lesson in maturity that related to that issue. Emotional healing is realized, which reduces the wounds from a feeling to a fact. A final rebirth occurs that leads into a dimming or forgetting of the past wound.

There are certain memories not forgotten until the major lessons become rooted and grounded within the healed individual. This is a lengthy process for many people due to the severity of the physical, emotional and mental damage of the past. Regardless of severity, healing takes time to complete and is based solely on the individual.

Only God can help an emotionally broken person, and they must learn how to fix their Self. This is where space, time and life experience affect this process. The one in crisis must learn by trial and error, just like everyone else, which is life's script in action.

Chapter 10

The midlife affair has nothing to do with the left-behind spouse and everything to do with the midlife spouse.

The midlife affair and affair partner are the most focused upon aspect of the crisis and are the most difficult mental and emotional hurdles to overcome for those who have not learned that the behavior of their spouse is not about them. Immaturity drives the affair, and the choices made to destroy the marriage were made by the midlife spouse, not the left-behind spouse.

Yet, the left-behind spouse internalizes this unwanted behavior thinking they have done something to cause the affair. That is not true. The midlife affair is about the midlife spouse who has made the decision to cross an emotional line and seek to use an outside solution to fix an internal problem.

This section deals with aspects of the midlife affair. Though explanations of the why and how aspects of adultery are included, it is not condoned.

In this chapter, we cover these topics:

- Emotional Imbalance
- The Search for Outside Solutions
- The Children of their Issues | Affair
- Core Character Compromised
- Brief Overview of the Midlife Affair
- Cake-Eating

- The Marriage Breakdown

Emotional Imbalance

The foundation of the midlife crisis is one of being emotionally unsettled, dissatisfied, and discontent. A person can have a strong mind but a weak temperament[1]. What is within the heart, the mind will usually follow unless mental shields, rendering it impervious to temptation of the emotions, protect that same mind.

People look too much toward feelings, put too much emphasis on material possessions, and their envious ways lead into a hard fall. They have not learned to be content within their circumstances. Their marriages are unsatisfying, but instead of looking within to see what can be done to bring change and renew the connection, most people seek a new relationship. New partners cannot fix old problems, because the problem is not in the partner. The problem is in Self, and these aspects are emotionally based.

When the emotions are in chaos and not brought into control, the strength of mind can be compromised. Most people do not bother to learn that, because looking within is too scary and too difficult. So, they think they can prowl for something better. Their perception is wrong. One cannot find something better because their own brokenness, lack of learning, growth, and logical thinking dictates that leaving a good spouse in a quest may cost them everything. However, they are selfishly consumed and not thinking logically. They are not happy, so a void they seek to fill ends with terrible actions that torture them from the inside out.

---

[1] This is a type of imbalance Satan dearly loves to exploit.

The Search for Outside Solutions

The best way to fully resolve their issues would be for the midlife to look within to answer the questions they face in this time of emotional unrest. However, because they were taught to look outward for solutions, their resulting identity crisis triggers an outward quest for who they are, outside of being within any relationship. Why? Because they believe their current relationships, including their marriage, are to blame for how they feel. So, they feel they must leave their present relationships in all aspects: emotionally, mentally, and to a certain extent, physically. Be assured, no outside solution can ever fix an inside problem.

Regardless of the kind of spouse the one in crisis has, their spouse could never be the cause of issues within their crisis. Even if married for a long time, the midlife crisis was in creation during their childhood, rooted and grounded within the life of their past. What one does not break, one cannot fix. One can only choose to release the one in crisis to figure out how to fix Self.

This is a physical, emotional, mental, and spiritual battle that can only be faced and fought by the individual in crisis. This crisis has nothing to do with anyone they may be associated with, including their spouse. The emotionally broken midlife spouse is searching for something they have missed. It is something the left-behind spouse is not able to provide. In addition, the left-behind spouse has never provided them with anything they were not given as children.

The Children of their Issues | Affair

Because the midlife spouse believes their marriage is to blame for how they feel, their heart and mind are turned away from the left-behind spouse. The inner child currently in control of the midlife spouse is the one that starts and maintains the affair that destroys everything. Until that same affair runs its course, and their heart and mind are turned back toward the left-behind spouse, there is nothing that can be done about the affair.

Full emotional regression occurs within their emotional psyche, which involves the most heavily damaged emotional child. There is unfinished emotional business within their past they are being forced to attend to because their emotional maturation was halted during their childhood and did not complete.

The affair partner often represents one or both parents and usually represents the most painful issues surrounding this same aspect. Some midlife spouses choose to go home to their parents because they have unfinished emotional business in this area. However, in the absence of the parents or because going home is too unbearable, an affair partner will serve as a stand-in.

One of the main goals of the emotional affair is to recreate a time of unconditional love that wasn't satisfied in childhood. Failing that, there is also a matter of an unbroken emotional connection on the part of the midlife spouse that should be broken. When they left home as young adults, most never made the emotional break required to render them emotionally independent. This break is the final step into adulthood. It doesn't require the parents to do anything; the ability to make this break lies upon the young adult.

If the emotional break from the parents isn't completed, the young adult will carry this same attachment into midlife. This attachment is at the root of adults who cannot let go of their parents, continue to be emotionally bound to them, and cannot relate to them as adults. This is one of the past issues a midlife spouse will face and must complete.

<u>Core Character Compromised</u>

The person in crisis is <u>not</u> usually looking for sexual contact.[1] They are looking to re-live or re-forge an emotional connection denied long ago. They are looking for validation of their pain, mirrored in another, seeking emotional connection that leads to comfort. As they seek to be accepted, they subconsciously search for someone just like them, someone lacking judgment and accountability found in normal relationships.

The affair partner will introduce sex into the connection to keep the midlife spouse from escaping the emotional affair. This introduction not only transforms the emotional affair into a physical affair, it also traumatizes the child within and creates more emotional damage.

As a result, their behavioral problems become worse, as they struggle with this fall from grace most did not intend. After it happens,

---

[1] Exception comes up if the midlife crisis includes a sexual complication and/or sexual addiction.

the struggle within intensifies as further destruction of their character occurs. Nothing a left-behind spouse does in retaliation can be worse than what the person in crisis has done to Self in the way of emotional damage.

This damaged inner child exhibits behaviors that correct past emotional errors made by their parent(s), and searches for the unconditional love never received as a child. It searches to fill that emptiness in Self that perceived it was never loved. This is the same behavior that drives the midlife spouse to divorce their left-behind spouse and marry their affair partner (aka their mistake). The state of mind of the midlife spouse is a combination of two factors:

- The brain fog caused from a chemical change triggered their depression state and does not go away when they divorce and remarry.
- The children of their issues drive their behavior to extreme limits.

The midlife affair that would clearly be adultery to the core personality is not seen as an affair or adultery to the child. Why? Because the child in control is struggling with their unfinished developmental processes.

Because Satan gets involved, their fall into temptation takes them further than they ever wanted to go. In the long run, it will cost them more than they ever wanted to pay.[1]

---

[1] For more on this, see Chapter entitled "The Consequences of Sin" in Section 2.

Brief Overview of the Midlife Affair
==========

Long before the midlife affair was conceived, the heart and mind of the midlife spouse turned a different direction as they began navigating through a world comprised of opposite behavior[1]. For the first time in their life, the midlife spouse desired an emotional connection with someone, which is the basis of the quest for unconditional love not received as a child.

The left-behind spouse is not allowed to meet these needs for two reasons:

- Emotional permission was stripped away when the midlife spouse became the opposite of what they were.
- The left-behind spouse can no longer meet their needs, because their needs have become different. This is usually a temporary change on the part of the midlife spouse.

As they become different, the midlife spouse unconsciously seeks someone like them, and similar to, if not just like, one or both parents. Since broken attracts broken, they find a friend who is as selfish as they are. The friendship starts with the purpose of seeking an emotional connection. None of the midlife affairs are about sex, and most midlife spouses never intend to commit physical adultery against their spouse. But in time, certain personal and moral lines are crossed in the heart and mind. Temptation draws them into the trap of physical adultery with whispered promises that can never be

---

[1] This emotional change for the opposite that occurs within the midlife spouse is not a valid excuse for seeking someone else without resolving the current relationship first.

kept, and things spin out of control in a way they never meant to happen.

As infatuation blinds their eyes, the midlife spouse only sees the good things in the affair partner. As the infatuation hormones rise, completely obscuring the emotional sight of the midlife spouse, they view the affair partner as the only person who understands and loves them.

Cake-Eating

When an affair begins, the spouse in crisis is caught between two people: their spouse and their affair partner. They have an onset of deep confusion and a genuine desire to be with both people because the affair partner meets some needs while the left-behind spouse meets other needs. This creates a best of both worlds' aspect.

To hide their secret life and avoid serious fallout, the midlife spouse splits their life into two different aspects and does everything possible to keep those two worlds from colliding. The midlife spouse seeks to stack the emotional deck in their favor, having the whole of their needs met while only meeting half the needs of the two partners. This is selfish and disrespectful toward both the left-behind spouse and the affair partner. The term cake-eating is defined as the attempt to take advantage of a situation that is morally wrong, seeking the best of both worlds without having to choose. It is more commonly known within the context of being married and having an affair partner as "having one's cake and eating it too."

Compartmentalization, though touted as a way of emotionally coping with this secretive way of cake-eating, is faulty in its emotional construction. The harder one tries to keep these situations separated; the more likely mistakes will occur. It's only a matter of time before the two worlds collide with a bang.

The Marriage Breakdown

It is selfish behavior to make sure one is never alone, while abandoning another. Especially when one is within a committed lifetime relationship, as marriage is meant to be. However, during the midlife crisis, the last thing on the midlife spouse's mind is their marriage. In fact, they set this major relationship aside at the earliest opportunity. They do not grieve the marriage they have destroyed, because they have not resolved it, nor are they emotionally or mentally finished with it. The marriage that existed before is dead to them, and within their minds, they are no longer married, and their commitment is broken in half.

The evidence of the marriage breakdown is in the midlife spouse's entitlement attitude, which tells the left-behind spouse in word and action they are no longer married and will do what they want. They do and say anything to justify the breakdown of the marriage, because they are driven to end all commitments and responsibilities associated with this former relationship.

Whether or not they expose the ongoing affair, they try to manipulate the left-behind spouse into asking them to leave. They want to leave and need their space to figure Self out, but responsibility for their decisions haunts them. They know if they leave, they are responsible, but if the left-behind spouse asks them to leave, they have justification for their rebellion against their marriage.

Some deliberately expose the affair in hopes their spouse will throw them out, giving them the perfect excuse and justification to move in with the affair partner. They think they are doing the right thing, yet do not realize they are gambling on an affair partner who will turn on them in due time. In addition, the midlife spouse does not realize the left-behind spouse may not wait on the affair to run its course and instead choose to permanently close the door to their return.

The confusion on the part of the midlife spouse about staying or leaving is indication they have not thought through their rebellion. It is also an indication they are in an emotional crisis driving them down a road they can never reverse. As a result, the midlife spouse, so sure in their wrong decisions, continues to engage in an affair that will cause more trouble than imagined. They have no idea what they will lose until later, when they awaken to what they have done.

Response of Left-behind Spouse to the Midlife Affair

- Leave the midlife spouse alone, placing them in the hands of God and praying for them. Step back and let them fall on their face.
- Set firm boundaries against bad behaviors.
- Focus on Self and create a life that does not include the midlife spouse. The choice does not have to be made to walk away from the marriage. But as time moves forward, walk

the road to wholeness and healing for Self, finding ways to adjust and adapt to the situation for emotional survival and mental sanity.
- Push fear away, trusting God to lead the way through this journey.
- Do not expose the affair; this will decrease the chance that the midlife spouse will return and destroy the inner trust the midlife spouse holds for the left-behind spouse.
- Refuse to believe the affair partner has it all. The one who lacks love and respect (the midlife spouse) cannot and will not give love and respect.
- The total blame for the beginning of the affair is on the midlife spouse. Don't get stuck in misdirected anger toward the affair partner. The midlife spouse broke their marriage vows.
- Work through the emotions about the affair and reach forgiveness for both parties, then let it go. The past cannot be changed, but one can look to the future, which can be changed.
- Most midlife spouses tempted into an affair never had the intention of leaving their marriage, which is one of the reasons the left-behind spouse is advised to back off, detach and distance from the midlife spouse and let the affair run its course.

Chapter 11

We stand at a crossroad every day, choose for better or for worse,
then live out the consequences of our choice.

In the preceding chapter, a brief overview of the midlife affair was given. In this chapter, we take a broader and deeper look inside and will cover the following topics:

- Choice of the Midlife Spouse to Stay or Leave
- The Stages of an Affair
- Timeline for the Affair
- The Affair Partner
- Infatuation is not Unconditional Love
- The Foundation of the Affair
- Masks and Mirroring Behavior
- The Affair Addiction
- Encouragement | The Strange Connection

Choice of the Midlife Spouse to Stay or Leave

Deep within their heart, the midlife spouse knows they will never find anyone like the left-behind spouse. Their feelings, still there, are buried under layers of justification that support their wrong actions against Self, their family and marriage. They must come to terms with their marriage and decide if the cost of staying outweighs the loss in leaving and starting over.

Though the crisis has overlaid their personality, they understand the immense loss if they choose a path away from the marriage. For some, the loss is too much to face, and they return home. For others, their fear of facing the damage created seems too much to overcome and they make the choice to leave. This marital relationship becomes a major emotional issue during the crisis because it is an issue the midlife spouse must face and decide to keep or discard. This is solely their decision. Every midlife spouse who has sought to fix their inside issues by creating a new life has lived to regret their decision. There is always a cost to pay, and each person must determine if their decision is worth the sacrifice and destruction of their character. The better choice is to walk the harder road that leads to eventual peace and happiness of experiencing full emotional maturity.

The Stages of an Affair

The road of every affair progresses and ends the same. Below are the most standard aspects that lead down this road of Self-destruction for both people involved. There are many different nuances, but this explains the main points.

Stage 1.

There is a chance meeting to get acquainted, though not recognized at first. There is no set place to meet a person that can[1] later become an affair partner; it can occur at work, church, in the grocery store, etc. Time is spent together, whether in person, phone calls, or social media. At some point, a personal line is crossed, and an emotional bonding is achieved. This results in infatuation because emotional needs are met by one through the other, and they fall in "luv"[2].

Stage 2.

More lines are crossed as human justification takes the place of Godly morality. Two broken people come together to use one another and avoid their Self. As time passes, much damage is done against one another.

Stage 3.

One or both people awaken to what they have done. If and when this happens, they may discover they don't like each other, and a crossroad of change and decision is faced. Misplaced responsibility begins, also known as emotional addiction, accompanied with guilt, shame and blame. Negative cycling comes next as either one or both people can't make the harder decision to let go. Emotional threats begin, including blackmail, tantrums, anger, and desperation to hold on to what one doesn't want to release. Breaking up is hard to do. The couple break down many times and come back together.

---

[1] I say "can" because every person has a choice.
[2] "Luv" is not true love. It is selfish, stays on the surface, and temporary in nature.

Each time, the situation grows worse as the emotional addiction is mistaken for commitment.

<u>Stage 4.</u>

Another crossroad of change and decision is faced for either one or both affair partners. Each person must decide if the pain involved in staying is worth the risk, or if the reward of leaving is greater than the pain in staying. When the pain of staying becomes worse than the pleasure of walking away, one person will make the choice. In many situations, the pain of staying must become the deciding force to leave, because when the pain becomes heavy enough, that person will do something about it. Even if it means abandoning the perceived source of that pain.

Pain can be a motivator because no one willingly withstands pain for long before deciding to change their circumstances. Ultimately, what is seen, felt and experienced is what drives one person away from the affair[1]. Hopefully the breakdown leads to examining the wrongdoing, thinking, and being that caused the trouble. In addition, the increased pain from the breakdown will be perceived as the fault of the affair partner.

<u>Timeline for the Affair</u>

Some midlife affairs last twenty-four months; others can last three to five years, if not longer. It depends on how quickly the affair partner loses their appeal, as well as how quickly the infatuation

---

[1] The affair which never served either one of them and only brought destruction to both.

hormones subside, dissolving the mask on both people. The length of the affair is also based on the midlife spouse's issues related to parental aspects and the seriousness of same.

Not only that, but the total length of the midlife crisis also hinges on whether the left-behind spouse is willing to focus on Self and give the midlife spouse space to work through their issues, including the affair. The more pressure a left-behind spouse puts on a midlife spouse to end their affair and return home, the closer the midlife spouse clings to the affair partner and insists on staying where they are. This can lengthen the time of both the affair and crisis.

Remember, the midlife affair is one of the running behaviors and a hallmark of the third stage, Total Emotional Regression. The third stage is a re-creation of their childhood, and reveals the issues of the midlife spouse, but those issues won't begin resolving until the fourth stage[1]. The affair partner cannot survive beyond stage three for two reasons:

- The midlife spouse must outgrow their need for the emotional addiction, called the midlife affair, used to avoid Self. The issue that drove them to the affair will be faced in the fourth stage, and the midlife spouse cannot enter that stage with the affair partner "in tow".

- The final three stages, should the midlife spouse get that far, will take every bit of their emotional energy to navigate.

---

[1] In the fourth stage, they are stripped of all pride and arrogance, and see their true SELF. No distractions are allowed during this time.

The Affair Partner

As previously discussed, the midlife affair is subconsciously set-up to help settle various issues within the midlife spouse. It is not unusual for the midlife spouse to recreate, relive or even replay a time in life that needs fixing or redoing. For this reason, the affair partner is usually like the midlife spouse's mother and/or father, or those who caused great emotional damage within the midlife spouse in childhood.[1]

Just as the midlife spouse has become the opposite of what they were before the crisis, their desires and needs take the opposite direction within Self. In a normal situation, opposites attract and likes repel. Within the realm of opposites, likes attract and opposites repel. So, the midlife spouse and affair partner are initially attracted to one another because they are alike. In fact, the affair partner is a negative reflection of the midlife spouse they are involved with[2]. The typical affair partner has suffered childhood damage from various abuses and emotionally unavailable people. Midlife spouses have suffered similar things, so each feed the issues within the other.

In addition, the affair partner is as broken as the midlife spouse. No emotionally healthy and self-respecting person engages in an affair with someone who is married or emotionally unavailable. They are a third party in what was meant to be a two-party relationship

---

[1] As discussed in Section 2, The Children of Their Issues.
[2] The affair partner is never a reflection of the left behind spouse.

between husband and wife. The fact they chose to be involved with someone unavailable reveals they have no morals, their character is broken, and they feel entitled to take what is not theirs. In a midlife crisis, neurotics attract neurotics and both partners look out for Self-interest, using one another to get what they want. In addition, it is common for the affair partner to suffer from various personality disorders, such as manic depressive, bi-polar, multiple personality disorders, and/or emotional instability. It is also common for the affair partner to be going through a midlife crisis.

All affair partners are emotional predators and a step down from the left-behind spouse. To commit any sin, one steps down to a lower level of morality. Those who engage in an affair with a married person walk in the gutter of their own morality. The affair partner has just as many, if not more, problems as the midlife spouse, but there should be a certain accountability that shows them to be just as immature, sinful and dishonorable as the midlife spouse who gets involved with them.

<u>Infatuation is not Unconditional Love</u>

The attempts of the midlife spouse to fill their need for unconditional love will fail. Neither the left-behind spouse nor the affair partner can meet the deeper emotional needs of the midlife spouse. Why? Because to emotionally connect, one must go beneath the surface to create emotional intimacy. The midlife spouse will not go down that road, because to connect emotionally requires full trust and the midlife spouse trusts no one – not even Self. They cannot accept Self, nor can they accept others. Any connection created is an addiction that is neither healthy nor mature. So, both the left-behind spouse and the affair partner will be held at arm's length or on the surface.

In the eyes of the midlife spouse, their affair partner is a perfect fit, or so they say. Negative comments made about the affair partner are met with the insistence they have found their soul mate. They protect the affair partner from harassment and claim the left-behind spouse drove them into the affair. To add insult to injury, the midlife spouse claims they are never returning home and file for divorce. Their excuse for filing? Their script includes "I've found the love of my life", "I've found my soulmate," "God wants me to be happy," or even, "God sent me this person." None of this is true. As they speak the script, their eyes seem to shine with an unnatural brightness one would see in a child who receives a new toy.

Indifference and cruelty are shown toward the left-behind spouse with statements such as, "Get over it; I don't love you anymore." The response of the left-behind spouse is devastation, despair, and the belief they have been replaced. They accept and carry the projected blame, shame and guilt. Yet none of this is true. The midlife spouse speaks from eyes blinded by the sheer exhilaration of infatuation, which has taken hold.

During this time, the affair partner is silent, wanting to be seen as the better option, a soft landing, strength, and "tru-luv". The affair partner doesn't argue, harp or pressure them. In fact, they encourage the midlife spouse to be irresponsible, as they give admiration, affirmation and acceptance, making them feel special, wanted, one of a kind, and desired, hanging onto their every word. The affair partner gives the midlife spouse their full, undivided attention and doesn't allow anything to come between them and their "true luv", their "soulmate". There is no judgment nor accountability, nor any reason to justify chosen actions. Both are completely blind to the reality of each other because they are both deep in the throes of infatuated love.

The Foundation of the Affair

In the affair both people use one another for different reasons. The midlife spouse uses the affair partner to make them feel special. The affair partner uses the midlife spouse for materialistic stability. Neither is aware of the other's agenda, and the affair never goes below the surface where all emotional needs are located. This is a teenage-type relationship made up of controllers and manipulators, and neither person knows what true love is.

The affair itself is built upon a weak foundation of lies, deceit, emotional masks and distorted reflections. The fantasy infatuation doesn't come close to meeting the emotional needs. It is often confused with love when, in fact, it is conditional love. In addition, the infatuation is shallow and equal to using and abusing the affair partner to make Self feel better. The infatuation turns into an emotional addiction, which is often mistaken for commitment. Emotional addictions are not true, honest nor honorable, nor do they build a strong relational foundation.

Masks and Mirroring Behavior

The midlife spouse and affair partner often mirror one another's behavior to avoid accountability. Because the foundation of an affair is built upon deception, both people only show what they want the other to see. These relationships are nothing more than the mirroring of a teenage romance. There is no love, dedication, mirror of accountability, honesty, openness nor trust between them.

There is the "other-based" mask imposed on the affair partner that enables the midlife spouse to evade, avoid, and escape the reality of the person they are entangled with. Because the affair partner is not always an exact and perfect fit, the midlife spouse makes use of a projected type of mask to compensate for what is lacking. It is an attempt to remake the affair partner into perfection, as opposed to accepting imperfections. When the time is right and past issues have been resolved, the mask projected upon the affair partner slips off, exposing the affair partner fully. This is due to the various changes within the midlife spouse's state of mind, and a readiness to move forward within the crisis.

As the midlife spouse faces the various children of their issues, they wear masks. While the left-behind spouse was used by the midlife spouse to take the brunt of the emotional unrest (spewing, anger, arrogant justification), the affair partner was used for fun, escape and avoidance of the midlife spouse's problems. Because these masks are used at the discretion of the midlife spouse, the affair partner is not exposed to the true colors of the midlife spouse. At the breakdown of the affair, the dissolving of said mask reveals the cruelty the midlife spouse kept hidden for the duration of the affair.[1]

Once these masks completely dissolve, the affair moves toward a time of final breakdown. Yet guilt, shame and the addictive properties of the affair cause the time of complete breakdown to increase. Time is one factor within the dissolution of the masks.[2] The other factor is a willingness to outgrow the self-deception necessary to maintain each kind of mask worn or projected by the midlife spouse.

The Affair Addiction

Once emotional infatuation fades, it transforms into a mental and emotional addiction. While within an affair, the midlife spouse is addicted to these four emotional highs:

- They had no responsibility within the area of the affair. The affair partner did not harp on them about bills and children. The affair represented fun and games.
- The affair partner made them feel special and needed, with lots of attention and little demands.
- They experienced teenage hormonal highs with the affair partner and the secrecy of the affair brought its own highs.
- When they were fighting, that had its own highs as well as teenage behaviors exhibited within both affair partners.

---

[1] The left behind spouse always knew the cruelty was there, because it was shown to them at the time of the unwanted emotional bomb drop.
[2] Both the Private and Public Mask as explained in Chapter 9, and the Affair Partner Mask described above.

Mental, emotional and physical abuse is present in every midlife affair. Jealousy, insecurity, and the clear inability to commit shows as the affair takes more work to stay together. But in public, the couple are a united force, paranoid of losing each other. This relationship has no boundaries nor Self-respect on either person's part. These relationships are not emotionally mature but rather more like teenage drama.

More Responses of Left-behind Spouse to the Midlife Affair

- Step back and allow the affair to run its course. This affair is not about the left-behind spouse.
- Back off, detach, and leave it alone. Focus on Self.
- Do not react, push, pressure or pursue the midlife spouse.
- Do not try to control or manipulate the situation; this makes matters worse.
- Do not contact the affair partner.
- Do not discuss the affair or affair partner with the midlife spouse.
- Do not try to break up the affair; it will play out in time.
- Do not believe anything the midlife spouse says about the affair partner.
- The only person one can control is Self. Not the midlife spouse nor the affair partner.
- The midlife crisis is about the midlife spouse. It is their journey to take. No one can fix them.
- The left-behind spouse is never responsible for the decision of the midlife spouse to have an extramarital affair.
- Set boundaries to limit contact to this affair.

- Use life lessons and survival skills of "Boundaries," "No Contact," "Detachment," and "Distance."[1]
- Any explanation given to children should be age related. Remember, it is never good to show the midlife parent as the enemy.

---

[1] More information about these aspects for the left behind spouse in Section 4, Survival Skills.

Chapter 12

In time, all of God's plans fall into place. All things are possible if you just believe and have faith in Him who knows the whole of your future.

The Affair Breakdown

Affairs are not meant to last because they are built on the foundation of avoidance, addiction, and emotional immaturity. Because each person only shows what they want the other to see, the typical affair is also rife with deception, lies, and secrecy and carry the elements of disrespect, emotional addiction, using, abusing and misusing. There is no accountability, no judgment, and no changing, growth or becoming what God intended.

The affair is a symptom, not the root cause, and generally there are various issues within the midlife spouse that fuel the affair. Once these issues are faced and settled, the affair partner is no longer needed. Infatuation, which cannot last forever, slowly gives way to dissatisfaction as the affair breaks down and the midlife spouse sees themselves clearly mirrored within the affair partner. At that point, the affair partner is seen as the one who dragged the midlife spouse into the relationship. Because the midlife spouse wishes to be considered a good person, they demonize and project the affair partner with their weaknesses, shortcomings, and failures to escape the reality of their part in the affair. While it does not help to blame the affair partner, this can help the midlife spouse gain the necessary strength to end the affair, as the affair partner shows their true colors, and the left-behind spouse begins showing as the better option. As the midlife spouse changes and turns away from the affair partner, emotional detachment[1] comes into play as the affair breaks down.

Though affairs do not begin or end immediately, the affair breakdown is always sudden and never easy. There is no gradual turning away, and the ending is emotionally violent with a great deal of drama leading to the end, assuming there is one. The affair partner rebels against the unwanted change, creating drama and pursuing, arguing, and using guilt to keep the midlife spouse. They cling, beg, plead and grieve[2], often luring the midlife spouse back for another round. In time there is a final break. Regardless of what the midlife spouse says, the breakup is never by mutual agreement.

The total drama that results is designed to teach the midlife spouse a hard lesson, so this mistake never repeats. It's not enough to just exit the affair; there must be an incentive given and lesson learned that is not easily forgotten.[3] There are serious consequences for

---

[1] This emotional detachment is similar to what happened with the left behind spouse.

[2] These are the same behaviors exhibited by the left behind spouse when the midlife spouse unexpectedly dropped the emotional bomb. The difference is the left behind spouse attained the tools for the journey, whereas the affair partner did not learn these things. Within a given time, they will get into another affair with someone else, repeating the same patterns.

[3] Once the fault within is processed and the issues finished, learned and settled, this event will be among many forgotten after the crisis is done.

affairs, and part of these are the mess involved in getting rid of the affair partner.

Each affair is different in the steps of breaking down, and sometimes the break is not completed until the midlife spouse makes a conscious decision to return home. However, because the person in crisis does not want to be alone, this necessary and permanent break may not be completed until after they return home.

Note: The affair always ends in the third stage, Total Emotional Regression. If the affair is ongoing, the midlife spouse is still in stage three.

Breaking the Affair Addiction

When the affair ends, emotional depression hits the midlife spouse. The infatuation gave the relationship a sense of hope in the beginning, but that hope fades, leaving addiction in its place. In the emotional battle[1] to break said addiction, an even deeper depression shows because the drug of choice (the affair partner) has been removed.

For the midlife spouse to release the mental and emotional addiction, all contact with the affair partner must stop. To ease their withdrawal symptoms and their guilt for dragging the affair partner into their mess, they are driven back multiple times. Therefore, they are often defensive and protective of the affair partner. They also miss

---

[1] This process of fighting and overcoming the addiction to the affair partner is a separate aspect from the depression experienced in stage 4, Facing Total Failure, which is a deeper depression.

the affair partner – more for what they did for them than the actual person, but they have associated and attributed their addictions, highs, etc., to this person. So, they grieve various emotions and feelings, including dealing with what was within Self that drove them to the affair. They feel guilt and shame knowing they must drop the affair partner, but for a time, weakness holds them back. Each time they make the break, the withdrawal symptoms cycle back to the beginning pains. Until they are emotionally ready to completely break down the affair, and it has become unsatisfactory to them, they remain cycling in this status quo.

The final break comes when enough emotional strength is gained to overcome their emotional triggers and navigate the grieving process into full acceptance of "what once was, will never be again." They must purge the existing connection with the affair partner from their head and heart. (Only then will the midlife spouse possibly turn back toward the left-behind spouse.)

Anytime an emotional connection is made with someone, whether moral or immoral, that person lays claim to the head and heart[1]. When the connection or relationship ends, this is grieved and processed.

The grieving process against the immature addiction is a hard burden to carry and involves the following:

- Grieving the end or loss of the affair and the affair partner.

---

[1] It is like the grief the left behind spouse faced at the death of the marriage, except the left behind spouse did not break an addiction, but rather experienced a loss of relational connection the midlife spouse destroyed when they set off the emotional bomb.

- Processing the shame and guilt of the addiction they once felt that drove them to the affair.
- Processing the meaning of the connection they forged with the affair partner, even though they knew they were wrong.
- Processing the addiction itself to rid themselves of it.
- Anger against the affair partner for leaving them when they "needed them most." Their anger over abandonment must be worked out because it is combined with immature jealousy.

After processing the lost connection, the true colors of the affair partner come to light, and memories of emotional red flags confirm the break up was the right thing. The midlife spouse realizes what they ran to was worse than what they ran from. They feel foolish and cannot understand how the affair partner they thought was good turned out to be bad. This truth eventually leads the grieving midlife spouse into demonizing the affair partner as they realize they have been "had, used and abused". This helps them purge the heart and head connection that led down the road of adultery and self-destruction. This takes time to work out.

Within the withdrawal, the connection is processed, broken, and purged from their head and heart, because they are done with the affair partner. The midlife spouse knows there is no going back. This must occur and end before the midlife spouse turns back to the left-behind spouse, based on the buried feelings that uncover as the grieving process ends.

Note: It is wrong to assume that just because the affair ends, marital rebuilding begins. At the breakdown of the affair, the midlife spouse may try to offload their guilt, shame and blame onto the left-behind spouse. The betrayal of Self and their spouse was their choice, and they must live with the emotional fallout they caused. The left-behind spouse is advised not to interfere or accept responsibility for their choices.

<u>The Strange Connection</u>

There is a "strange connection", unbreakable and maintained, between the married couple, despite the ongoing affair. It is a connection the affair partner will never have. The midlife spouse becomes aware of this connection that draws them toward the left-behind spouse, earlier abandoned for perceived greener pastures.

Though the midlife spouse may be in an affair, after a period, an emotional shift begins that leads to two things:

- A changed perception.

Just as their feelings and perceptions changed earlier to justify their affair, they experience a return of feelings causing them to perceive the positive aspects in the spouse they left-behind, now seen as the greener pastures.

- An internal awakening to circumstances within the affair.

As the midlife spouse awakens within the context of the affair, they perceive the left-behind spouse moving away from them, which is an unwanted move for most people in crisis. Believing their illusion of control over the left-behind spouse has been disrupted or shattered can be enough to move them toward ending the affair, whether they return home before or after. The awakening triggers a major perception of their personal loss.

Once the midlife spouse awakens to their mistake and the situation rolls in reverse, the left-behind spouse should be in a position of showing strength, being the soft landing necessary to draw the midlife spouse back. As the process moves forward, the affair partner will be in the position the left-behind spouse once stood in, with the midlife spouse treating them as coldly as they once treated the left-behind spouse. It's not possible to be in love, or to love two people in the same way – there can only be one true love.

Because of history, children, and a long-standing marital life that includes a familiarity with the left-behind spouse, it is more likely the midlife spouse will return to the marriage to try again, if the left-behind spouse will allow them to do so.

After Effects of the Affair

People who have affairs damage their character and their inner Self. At some point, they lost self-respect. It is a lot to overcome, but it can be done through the power of God and the steadfast love of the left-behind spouse. The aftereffects of adultery carry consequences. Those are covered in the chapter, "The Consequences of Sin."

Chapter 12

The Truth shall set you free, but Deception will keep you bound.

The core character is comprised of three major components, linked together in a never-ending circle: integrity (to be honest), morality (to be upright) and empathy (to be compassionate). One cannot have integrity without exercising morality and empathy; one cannot have morality without exercising integrity and empathy; one cannot have empathy without exercising integrity and morality. All three components are tested during times of trial, as temptation springs forth[1]. Satan is successful with 99.9% of midlife spouses. It only takes a fall from one of these components to fall into sin. All temptations begin with the intent to destroy the core character within the one tempted-one aspect at a time.

Everything done, whether right or wrong, originates from within Self. Selfishness will cost a person more than they can ever recover once their integrity has been compromised to dishonesty. One must navigate the harder aspects to reach full resolution of Self. But to the midlife spouse, it is too hard to walk the rocky road of Self, learning to navigate the obstacles that lead to a positive outlook. So, they look for the perceived easy way out, taking the first detour they see, which is Satan's trap. Every detour dead-ends at an emotional

---

[1] Satan cannot read minds or hearts, but he can read our countenance (facial features) and sends temptation to attack the midlife spouse through their emotional unrest and immaturity.

cliff, which results in destruction as they walk off the edge where they face the death of a former honorable aspect they once held within their character, whether it be integrity, morality or empathy.

The Venture into Sin

There are four steps that venture into sin; sin doesn't happen all at once.

- To be tempted down a given path that leads into the committing of any sin, we must first expose Self to the thought, which is filtered through our core character before further steps are taken.
- The second step is working the thought out within the mind. Rationalization and justification desensitize the mind and gives permission to move ahead with the temptation.
- The third step is to carry out the temptation, after which one suffers the severe shock of having fallen into the trap of deception. For many people, this is enough to cause them to back down. For others, the addiction kicks in and keeps them chained for a season. This is the moral and emotional crossroad where decisions are made.
- The final step is dealing with the fallout. Once reality hits, the one who has fallen suffers painful losses and heavy consequences. Each time a person goes against their moral code, they are damaged in various ways, causing deep wounds which take time to heal.

Total loss is experienced in the final step. Scripture says, "The wages of sin is death."[1] In translation, this means loss is a consequence of our sin. Sin will take one farther than they ever meant to go and cost them more than they ever thought they would pay. This loss always happens at the end of the commission of sin.

God has compassion, but He also allows consequences for actions. Good or bad, it always returns to reaping what is sown[2]. This aspect is no different for the person in crisis.

Forgiveness and consequences are separate entities. God's forgiveness was never designed to remove the consequences that follow every sin committed. God speaks of reaping (consequences) what one has sown (actions that lead to consequences), but He is not specific on the time of a season nor how long it will be.

<u>The Trek into Adultery</u>

Although each betrayer is faced with the temptation of adultery or a variation of the same, (porn, strippers, etc.) each one has full knowledge of their actions. They can throw tantrums, attempt to escape responsibility and blame others, but when the layers of sin are stripped away, all that remains are the betrayer and the utter destruction they caused.

Though the midlife spouse bears full responsibility for their choice to engage in an affair, Satan uses this fallen affair partner as

---

[1] For the wages of sin is death. Romans 6:23
[2] Do not be deceived: God cannot be mocked. A man reaps what he sows.
[8] Whoever sows to please their flesh, from the flesh will reap destruction; whoever sows to please the Spirit, from the Spirit will reap eternal life. Galatians 6:7-8

emotional bait to draw the innocent down a path of destructive sin. This fall into temptation will destroy both the affair partner and the immature, unwary, undiscerning and mentally confused midlife spouse who has unwittingly given Self emotional permission to step outside of marriage to seek an outside solution that will never resolve an inside problem. But no one can do wrong and get by with it. It's the consequence of sin[1].

What goes around comes around is the main basis for their never-ending consequences. The human mind will always follow what is within the heart. So, God plants tormenting feelings of guilt, shame, and regret into the heart of a rebellious midlife spouse. Once planted, their minds does the rest. This is how God gets around the "free will" exclusion He created. Man has free will to decide, and God will not tamper with that, but God will use the emotions (the heart) to create one of the worst brands of emotional and mental hell that man has ever tried to survive. When God takes hold of someone like that, they are in for the long haul, until they straighten up or die trying.

The rebellious midlife spouse's future lot is a life of relenting and unending misery. They can ask God for forgiveness, and He does give it. But keep in mind, this torment of memories is not a retraction of His forgiveness, but rather a solid consequence for the sin committed. Within the fall into temptation, a certain innocence is lost that will never be regained. There is no going back to what once was; everything has changed because of one person's sin.

---

[1] When people choose the behavior, they also choose the consequences of that behavior.

There are consequences for actions perpetrated during and after the midlife crisis. There are consequences that happen all along the way that alert the sinner to the fact they are on a road toward Self-destruction. And for some, after the crisis ends, there will be lingering health consequences for some of the running behaviors.

The sinful life of the midlife spouse is not a bed of roses, rather of thorns. Darkness dogs their steps because they continually reap what has been sown in corruption. The consequences are always disastrous because problems always increase when they try to use outside solutions to fix inside problems.

The midlife spouse suffers the consequences for their actions against God, Self, spouse and family. A dark cloud follows the sinner. The only way to resolve the cloud is to examine and resolve Self and resolve the issues in full. God will only go so far before distancing from the sin a person is committing, releasing them to their own devices and eventually allowing them to fall on their fact to experience the harsh consequences.

God does not advocate, condone or otherwise overlook adulterous actions. For everything a person does, every sin they commit and every bit of dishonor they seek to visit upon the marriage they destroy, God ensures they suffer serious and severe consequences for their actions. They are miserable because no person on Earth can do wrong and get by with it.

The Dead End of Adultery

Adultery is wrong, according to God's Word, and people should work to maintain fidelity in marriage. Unfortunately, there are those who think the best solution to a problem in marriage is solved by stepping outside of marriage, committing emotional or physical adultery, and then blaming the left-behind spouse for their failure to keep the adulterer happy. Society buys into this wrong thinking.

The fault does not lay within the one who was cheated on, but on the one who is cheating. Yet the midlife spouse who steps into an affair blames the left-behind spouse for a weakness the left-behind spouse did not have control over.

The Consequences of Adultery

Reaping what one sows in corruption for what one has done brings forth death and consequences for a season. Long lasting guilt and shame brings about times of shock and amazement as the midlife spouse desperately and unsuccessfully tries to distance from what they have done. When the time is right, their emotional strength takes them into a place where their sin is shown to them, and they are forced to reconcile Self. The same person who spoke and committed fidelity, the same person who promised to love and cherish, instead abandoned their spouse in pursuit of their selfishness.

It is no wonder the midlife spouse cannot view the damage they have done in full. If the entire processing were given to them at one time, their fragile minds and emotions would snap like a slender stick. The mental and emotional health of the midlife spouse is extremely sensitive and weak during the post-affair time. They are struggling to process the affair for what it meant, trying to reconcile the person they are with the person they became for that period, and they won't completely reconcile Self until much later in the midlife crisis when their emotional and mental health are strong enough to do so.

Even then, it is hard for them. God will not put any more on them than they are strong enough to bear, as He holds them strictly accountable through their memories once He deems them strong enough to take this accountability.

It is later, as the horrifying reality of what they have done returns to haunt them, they realize they have sacrificed their entire life, Self, and marriage upon an altar of sin that cannot be erased. They know when they are crossing a forbidden line, hence the secrecy and deceit often exercised within the affair. However, they keep turning away from a certain mirror of reality, judgment and accountability because they want to continue avoiding facing Self.

In time, everything comes full circle, and their sin comes home to roost. One can run far and wide, but in time, what they have done will return to be accounted for. What they have done is between their dishonored Self and God. He will deal with them harshly as He makes certain they serve consequences that match the severity of the sinful deeds perpetrated.

This is not God punishing the midlife spouse, rather it is the midlife spouse suffering the consequences of their wrong actions as they sin against God and their left-behind spouse in ways designed by Satan to tear down what was built up over time.

What Satan means for our destruction, God will bring forth a glorious victory for and within those who learn to accept, forgive and heal from what has been done against them. However, once all accountability and consequences have been served, God doesn't bring this back up in the sinner's mind.

Consequences for The Affair Partner

What is sown in temporary pleasure will be reaped worse than the anger and pain dealt the left-behind spouse by the affair partner.

The breaking of their own emotional addiction upon the final split of the affair will always be more severe, as they are refused multiple times by the midlife spouse before they finally decide to stop pestering and harassing the midlife spouse who belonged to another by God's marital covenant.

Response for the Left-behind Spouse to the Consequences

- Do not try to protect the midlife spouse from the consequences of their sin. If this is done, the one who interferes will reap what was sown by the midlife spouse. Step back, let go, and let God work in them. He does His part in ensuring that no one escapes the consequences of their sin.
- Set aside vindictive and vengeful actions, words and thoughts. Let bitterness and unforgiveness go. It is not the role of the left-behind spouse to punish, control or manipulate the midlife spouse. These activities feed their justification for their rebellion against the marriage. Leave the midlife spouse in the hands of God.
- Guard against the attitude of self-victimization; resist the urge to bait, pursue, push and pressure the midlife spouse. Rather, accept responsibility for personal contributions to the unhealthy marriage that existed at the time of breakdown and continue the journey toward wholeness and healing.
- The left-behind spouse should not choose to personalize, internalize or even rationalize the sin of their midlife spouse. This is not a "couple" problem, it is an individual problem and involves one individual whose perception changed in a negative way. They chose and decided to abandon the marriage in favor of a new relationship they mistakenly thought would solve an internal problem. This

is their problem to live with and to work out.
- Never discount the power of God because God knows the heart, the need, and He knows exactly what to do to influence the consequential fall that always happens when sin is committed against an innocent person.

Chapter 13

Though painful, taken alone, and heartbreaking, this journey is a battle worth taking,
for the codependency is transformed into interdependency.

The Turn Toward Home

By the time their eyes turn toward home, the left-behind spouse has become the better option and the situation rolls in reverse. The affair partner pushes, pressures, pursues and threatens the midlife spouse, while the left-behind spouse maintains their distance and detachment, and their strength becomes an attraction. They shine a light that draws the midlife spouse home.[1]

In re-connecting, a backward path is taken. This path is based on the amount of destruction caused, and the real or perceived emotional threat the midlife spouse fears from the left-behind spouse,

---

[1] On the other hand, if the midlife spouse returns home to the left behind spouse who has not changed and pushes, pressures, and pursues, the midlife spouse will walk back out. The left behind spouse carries the responsibility for their own journey.

the children or even household pets. The path taken is about feeling safe. In the public aspect, it's not unusual for the midlife spouse to connect with former friends and then their extended family before moving toward home. From a private aspect, many times the first connection is with household pets, as they pose the least amount of threat. Next a connection is made with the children and finally with the left-behind spouse, who is last because of their emotional connection with, and the emotional damage caused in the relationship.

It is common for the midlife spouse to gradually sneak their way back into the household. Some begin the gradual process of visiting, staying longer and longer until they decide to return home. During this time, they test the emotional bridge for strength before deciding to cross. Sneaking often irritates the left-behind spouse (unless they are willing to deal with the small steps forward), because they want the midlife spouse to come home and account for themselves. This will not happen all at once. It never does. Why? If pressured to answer questions before they are ready, a midlife spouse who has no emotional awareness will become afraid and run away, cycling backward, and may or may not try again to return.

Patience is key during this time of watching them connect backward. It is best to build the connection and allow time for the connection to strengthen. Move slowly without pressuring, because the midlife spouse cannot take a fast-moving situation. When they move forward, fear is usually seen. Like a child who has done something wrong, afraid of repercussions, they often feel holding their head down will keep them safe.

The Return Home

Though loss is what drives the midlife spouse to return home, the left-behind spouse won't recognize it because the midlife spouse continually second guesses their decisions. They say they returned for financial reasons, the children, for anything except their spouse. Truth is, they return because they are afraid of losing the left-behind spouse and the life they once abandoned for their selfish wants and desires. In the mind of the midlife spouse, they are not sure what they want, but they do not want to raise hope. As a warning to the left-behind spouse, expectations are dangerous during this time.

All midlife spouses, should they attempt a new connection with the left-behind spouse, return during the end of the third stage, Total Emotional Regression. They return emotionally broken, in sore need of help so they can rebuild Self. Most midlife spouses still have the affair partner in the shadows because they are unable to be alone with Self. Some ask to return home, holding the unconscious hope the left-behind spouse will not only allow them to return, but also help them completely break down the affair. Others simply show up on the doorstep.

Their return comes at a time when the left-behind spouse has regained emotional balance, completed detachment and no longer has the midlife spouse at the forefront of their mind. In my experience, no left-behind spouse is ever ready for this to happen. The return of the midlife spouse threatens everything the left-behind spouse has built, because by this time, their life is peaceful, acceptance has been gained, strength is growing, and the adjustment to the former chaos has been accomplished.

This return always brings a crossroads of choice for the left-behind spouse – do they accept or reject the midlife spouse who has committed adultery, and perhaps still has the affair partner in the shadows? Are they willing to allow the midlife spouse, along with their chaos and drama, back into their lives in hopes of marital restoration? The left-behind spouse holds all the proverbial aces, as they know they don't have to allow this to happen. There are serious issues of trust, love, and fear knowing the midlife spouse could leave again if they are not ready to mend some of the damage.[1]

The Harder Work

Even after a return is achieved, the harder work begins. Not every situation follows the same script, so what comes next is a common scenario that shows and explains cake-eating in its reversal form.

If the left-behind spouse allows the midlife spouse to return home, the cake-eating aspect begins anew, with a twist. This time, the situation reverses as the focus turns back toward the left-behind spouse rather than the affair partner. As time moves forward, there are still emotionally addictive, misplaced responsibility tendencies toward the affair partner, and the same confusion experienced in the beginning must be fought and overcome.

The cake-eating aspect continues as the midlife spouse may try several times to end the affair, but the affair partner uses emotional blackmail to keep the midlife spouse, leading them to experience guilt and a false sense of responsibility.

---

[1] If the midlife spouse is turned away, one cannot blame the left-behind spouse for their decision.

One may be led by intuition to speak truth in forcing the hand of the midlife spouse to end the affair. Only the left-behind spouse knows a reasonable amount of time to give the midlife spouse to end the affair on their own. However, if no intervention is necessary, show love and acceptance, be a soft place to land, and be the better option when compared to an emotionally out of control affair partner. And under no circumstances should the left-behind spouse speak with the affair partner. Nothing productive would come from this. Any type of interfering would be described as an emotional mine field.

Tensions usually run high between the affair partner and the midlife spouse, and one does not want to share in the fallout. Bear in mind, the left-behind spouse did not start this affair, therefore, has no responsibility to help break it down.

As much negative drama as the midlife spouse is known to create, they simply cannot take pressure from the affair partner. So, the greater the negative drama between the midlife spouse and the affair partner, the more likely the positive outcome for the left-behind spouse. Some affair partners become so angry they overplay their desperate hand and lose everything. This is a totally desirable option, once the midlife spouse realizes the affair partner is simply not worth dealing with and all contact and cake-eating stops as the affair ends.

Once the affair has ended, the midlife spouse needs time and space to process what drove them down the path to adultery. Until the midlife spouse has gained personal insight into this, no real progress can be achieved. Why? Because it's human nature to avoid, evade and try to escape personal responsibility for what they have done to destroy the marriage. In addition, they will inform their left-behind spouse that the subject of the affair and the affair partner are off limits.

<u>Walking the Emotional Tightrope</u>

This is where the whole situation becomes a tightrope, because one cannot make another face Self, and pushing may result in one of the following:

- The midlife spouse may have a nervous breakdown that may result in suicide.
- The midlife spouse may decide to walk out again.
- The marriage results in divorce because the left-behind spouse pressed for details and accountability, and the midlife spouse was not ready to confront Self or share details.

Space and time are needed for the midlife spouse to process and work through their issues. The affair is about them and was not caused or forced by the left-behind spouse.

It is a fine balance to continue change, growth and becoming while continuing to deal with the midlife spouse. Changes in the left-behind spouse will trigger changes in the midlife spouse. Whether these changes are positive or negative will lie within the midlife spouse's chosen response or reaction. A situation usually becomes worse before it becomes better or begins to resolve. However, it takes time because resolution does not come overnight.

Making a connection without allowing Self to be drawn into unneeded and unwanted drama is the most difficult part for the left-behind spouse in walking the emotional tightrope. It would be easy to allow a past indiscretion that led to betrayal and hurt to color one's perceptions. Learning to separate the behavior from the person is important and knowing how to help the midlife spouse move forward requires intuition.

Slow Moves Forward

In time, the midlife spouse attempts to put everything back the way it was before they left. Why? Because the midlife spouse has not changed. But the left-behind spouse has changed and understands how to set firm yet loving boundaries against bad behaviors directly affecting them. The left-behind spouse knows not to put too many changes in place at one time but gradually implements boundaries. The role of a stanchion is to get the midlife spouse's attention in a positive way, not to push, pressure, pursue or threaten the midlife spouse who is still in a great deal of emotional pain.

At this point, compassion[1] is exercised and accountability is set aside in favor of patience and giving time needed for the midlife spouse to adjust to the left-behind spouse who is not the same person they left. The midlife spouse must be given continued time and space to grow. If the midlife spouse is not ready to deal with the changes made in the left-behind spouse, they may walk out.

---

[1] Compassion does not mean to condone one's sinful actions against another.

The leaving and returning cause upheaval within the household and demands an adjustment each way. Though the left-behind spouse follows their intuition, it is a difficult emotional adjustment because the midlife spouse is not finished with their crisis. They are still in the third stage of *Total Emotional Regression* and have been slowly realizing they cannot put everything back the way it used to be.

As the left-behind spouse changes and has changed, it will trigger changes in the midlife spouse. This is how this journey was designed in the first place. To learn to function within a relationship, one must learn about Self. This involves learning what one will and won't accept in the way of behavior from other people and learning to set appropriate boundaries designed to stop bad behavior. The left-behind spouse is called upon to lead by example, hence these same changes. It is the only way the midlife spouse will begin to grow up, should they choose to. For any differences to show within the midlife spouse, the left-behind spouse must orchestrate the changes with the help of God.

Because two people in a crisis have lessons to learn, no one is going to return home whole and healed without walking the rest of that road of learning. God does not heal ether spouse immediately. Both have a road of learning yet to walk, as each one triggers learning in the other.

And so, the return home is only the beginning of more work that must be done, and a much harder road to walk, as God continues to guide the left-behind spouse forward within the usage of their own intuition.

Reconciliation | It Takes Two

God performs marital restoration, but He does not do it overnight. Both people must walk the road of learning. There is no other way to finish a major trial without going through it, experiencing the lessons that come out of it, and moving into the healing process. These take time. Even after the midlife spouse returns, it takes time to rebuild trust, belief and faith with the left-behind spouse they wronged.

One of the most marked changes one can see within the midlife spouse is the learned ability to truly love in an unconditional way. Their world evolves around the left-behind spouse in ways not before seen. They become protective of the relationship, and instead of thinking about Self, they seek to understand and meet the spouses' emotional needs. They become interdependent rather than codependent, still retaining their individuality, while remaining part of a relationship. Their lives are separate, yet they clearly recognize their commitment to the person they married.

One also sees their willingness to take responsibility and ownership for their part of the damage done during the worst of the midlife crisis. They display a willingness to mend the broken fences from that time. These things are shown in part during the crisis itself, but once the crisis is exited by way of the Final Fears, a time of renewal, rebuilding and reconciliation leads into an attitude of, "I did this, I'm truly sorry. What can I do to ensure it doesn't happen again?"

No longer are they emotionally bound to their parents in unhealthy ways, they have learned the value of boundaries that not only affect Self and their immediate family, but also their extended family. The changes made also affect their relationships with others, their job, and even their friends, as they become stronger, more resolute, in control of their emotional reactions, using responses (rather than reactions). They also become even-tempered. Wisdom and knowledge may be gained as well. Once the healing is finished, they are settled, peaceful, gentle, kind and loving.

As the couple moves forward within the ongoing process of the reconciliation and the rebuilding of their marriage, they continue as before, working closely together to resolve all issues resulting from the recent crisis. Because of their ongoing joint efforts to heal their reconnected marital bond, a scar will eventually replace the earlier wound.

There are no steps given to help the married couple reconcile and rebuild the broken marriage. There are resources available, but marital dynamics of each marriage differ greatly. If both individuals have taken the journey to wholeness and healing, they should contain all that is necessary within to aid each other within these reconciliation and rebuilding phases.

There are no clear signs of an ending, just living life within a completely new way. Eventually, all memories within both people will purge, and in time no longer be present. Indeed, time does heal all wounds leading into a very peaceful existence.

There are also positives that can result in the marriage of the couple that has reconciled. Listed below are a few.

Positives for the Midlife Spouse

- They realize the best thing they ever had was standing in front of them all along – their left-behind spouse.
- Grace and forgiveness will eventually be extended to them from their betrayed spouse.
- Gains the clarity that comes with having made the biggest mistake of their life. This leads them to target the issue within that drove them down the road of adultery. This, in combination with the boundary set by the left-behind spouse against an affair ever happening again, drives the midlife spouse to get necessary help for Self.
- God becomes real to them. They seek and receive forgiveness. They must still face the consequences for the sin of adultery.
- Learns what commitment is, probably for the first time in their life.
- Achieves much needed growth in a positive direction. People who have affairs are immature.
- Once the eyes of the midlife spouse are opened to these things, there is no going back into ignorance again. This is true of both the midlife spouse and the left-behind spouse.

Positives for the Left-behind Spouse

- Awakened to problems within the marriage which triggered a journey toward wholeness and healing within Self. This is true regardless of whether the midlife spouse is present or absent.

- Sets boundaries post-affair, forcing the midlife spouse to communicate their needs to, and have them met, by the left-behind spouse.

Chapter 15

Change is difficult, growth is pain,
but the becoming that occurs is what makes the victim, a victor.

<u>Hearts Blessing | An Unwanted Journey</u>

Somewhere along the way of being a daughter, wife, and mother, I got lost. When I found myself on this road[1] the future looked uncertain, and the way ahead was a bank of fog. Moving forward into the unknown was a frightening prospect. Thus, began my own journey toward wholeness and healing, as I took the first step forward through the emotional trial that was triggered by my husband's midlife crisis.

Moving forward is not the same as moving on. Had I moved on, I would have left everything and not walked my journey. I would have traveled full circle to the beginning of where I was when forced on this road I never wanted. Moving forward was a more productive aspect.

I spent time deep within an emotional rut of my own misery, as I suffered several emotional breakdowns. Below are a few thoughts I struggled with:

- I thought I lost everything, when all I really lost was myself.

---

[1] A road I did not ask for, nor plan to take,

- I thought I was being directly damaged.
- I thought the crisis of marriage was my fault.
- I thought what had happened was within my control.
- I knew I was not given a choice in what happened.
- I grieved a broken connection that was ripped from me.

Everything had changed, and I had yet to discover this would bring positive change into my life. For all I knew, there was nothing else to live for. I thought no one understood how I felt. People tried to help me, but all I could hear was that I was the one who needed to change, and I could not understand why.

I was devastated, furious, blamed myself for what happened. I internalized every hateful thing he said. I bought into every lie he told. Everything was my fault. I thought, "If I am such a bad person, why did it take so long for this come out?" I internalized everything, which made me feel worse. It was as if I had caused all of this but was not given a chance to fix it. Additional blame, shame, and guilt were heaped upon my already broken shoulders. The more miserable I was, the more satisfied my midlife spouse seemed to be.

I carried a heavy emotional burden that combined my responsibility and contributions with his for the eventual breakdown of our marriage. As long as he was able to put his personal responsibility and contributions for the breakdown of our marriage on me, he could continue to distance himself from the problem, which actually existed within him. However, I did not know the truth in those early days. Months after I discovered our marriage was dead, I went into an emotional spiral that led into a deep depression. I could not eat, sleep, nor rest, and my mind would not shut down.

The Call to Change from the Inside Out

I heard God say it was time to make changes within Self, because if I didn't change, nothing would change, and the situation would get worse. But I didn't listen. Why?

- I did not know how to or want to connect with my inner Self, so the shield I used to prevent others from connecting with me became tighter. I was emotionally unavailable to my own Self, not just to other people.
- I was afraid to accept the fact that change was called for. I didn't want to investigate my past and start poking sleeping dogs because I didn't want to get bitten.
- I repeated one single question several times, "What am I supposed to change? My husband needs change more than I do."

Yet God persisted, sending people who told me, "God says you need to change to eventually bring forth change in your husband. He doesn't know how to change and since his mind is confused, fogged and clouded, and yours is not, you are the one who should learn to change yourself."

When I finally hit rock bottom, I realized I had to help myself. It was up to me to find a way out of this low emotional. The only way out was upward and onward. I needed to grasp this opportunity and do something productive with it. I was dealt a raw deal, but I could learn to turn it around. Had I remained where I was, in this emotional rock bottom, I would have only hurt myself. I thought no one cared, but God did. He intervened, influencing me away from my suicidal thoughts and leading me out of that dark, cold place.

He showed me the way and gave me help. Through His guidance, I found the beginning of my own journey that would lead me into eventual peace, but I knew it would take a long time to navigate.

The Internal Mirror of Reflection

God showed me the Internal Mirror of Reflection where I would make some of my greatest emotional discoveries and face some of my deepest heartaches. Before I could move forward, it behooved me to look back. I examined my past that stretched across 35 years into my earliest childhood memories. I recalled memories good and bad that shaped my life across that time.

What was I looking for? Pieces of the past that I could discover, pick up, examine honestly, and learn the lessons that were associated with each one. In time, I learned how to put these emotional pieces together, so I could make positive changes in my life.

The first issues were the ones that led me down the road into marriage. Who I thought I was, was not the person I became. There were different threads of emotional learning tracing back to the past issues I had never considered, examined, nor overcome.

It is interesting to note that when I began this journey, I had no idea I was so shattered. I knew my childhood was not ideal, but I didn't know my issues ran so deep within. In spite of everything endured throughout my life, I retained a positive outlook which spoke of being able to overcome the past hurts, lost dreams, a shattered self-esteem, and a destroyed self-confidence.

The Emotional Road of Hell

The Emotional Road of Hell traveled to arrive at peace was difficult and painful. Unhealed emotional memories and flashbacks from childhood to adulthood surfaced and had to be examined, understood and resolved before healing could come. Then every deceptive layer contained within Self was stripped away, and I suffered an emotional crisis that rocked me to my core. But I needed the shaking, because it was time to grow up, make changes, and account for my failure of being honest and true to Self. My life had been spent evading, avoiding, and trying to escape Self. These things were necessary to reach full closure of every past issue I discovered within Self, whether caused by me or others. It was time to become the emotionally mature adult God meant me to be.

It is possible to be at odds within Self. What you think you are and what you really are, are often two different stories. Like many people, I considered myself a good person, but I had a lot of growing up to do. Though it all took time, I am grateful for the road I was put upon, a road I did not ask for nor plan to take. Without it, I wouldn't be where I am now, still changing, growing and becoming what God means for me to be.

Walking This Journey in Grace and Understanding

I walk this road every day with different people from all walks of life, starting from one end and leading to the other, moving back and forth between one aspect in one person's journey to a different one in another person's journey. No two people are alike in how their journey progresses.

God continues to equip me across many different areas within this time of life in the midlife transition and the complementing journey to wholeness and healing. I teach about the midlife crisis for the purpose of increasing people's understanding, then nudge them toward their own personal journey.

Why? Because once they understand the midlife crisis in an ongoing way, there is nothing else they can do. So, they may as well take the time they have been given to learn to stand for themselves. With a love that is often tough along the way, I carry out my part by exposing them to knowledge and tools that are helpful to those who choose to utilize these for their own benefit.

Not every person comes out as successfully as I did. Most people do not want to do the inner work necessary to reach the place of inner peace. They want to arrive, but also want to bypass the work necessary to reach the end. That cannot be.

Most people do not want to hear how it is not enough to trust God, they must also learn to trust a process they perceive has damaged them. They do not want to hear that one must learn to change, grow and become through a personal process that is much life the midlife spouse's process. They often forgot the decision to continue the marriage, or walk away, was never theirs. That decision was made by their midlife spouse. These same midlife spouses often chose alternate paths that prolong their midlife crisis, or the left-behind spouse sabotages themselves by not taking the advice given.

This is one of life's biggest tests of faith. Faith isn't tested in easy situations; it's tested when a situation becomes uncertain and unstable. The pain causes one to cling to God as never before. Left-behind spouses come for help to save their marriage yet find they must first save Self. In the beginning of my own trial, God convinced me to Stand for my marriage, giving me a light of hope. But I still had to walk the harder road to get to the end of the trial.

Dedication

This section is dedicated to the left-behind spouse on a similar journey. The following pages contain tools, survival skills and life lessons for this path of growth, change and becoming. I encourage you to learn to use them for the betterment of your Self. Each person is different within the context of what is needed in the way of information to overcome and move forward. This is true whether the marriage stays separate or comes back together. God is the guide through this journey. Trust Him, lean into Him and allow Him to lead.

Chapter 14

This is your journey forward, if you choose to accept and rise to the challenge.
You have nothing to lose and everything to gain!

This section contains additional instruction, guidance, encouragement, tools for survival, and life lessons to provide insight and understanding into this journey of a lifetime. Push back stubbornness and fear, lean in to the teachings, and behold the work that can be done in the heart and life of a willing student who desires to walk this path forward into wholeness and healing.

Thus, It Begins with You

Since very few people will move forward into a painful journey[1] on their own, they are forced into it by circumstances beyond their

---

[1] In this writing, we refer to the journey taken at the break in relationship. There is also a transitional journey one faces at midlife that does not become a crisis. Both journeys involve crossing over into the negative side of Self. The transitional journey takes it further because it not only involves the past marital relationship, it involves all relationships, all time and seasons of a person's life. This transitional journey forces a deeper self-examination, and extracts a change, as it burns many things from a person, forcing them to go through a stage of change. This change involves the disintegration of Self which leads toward a time of reintegration and rebirth that renders them changed and different than they were before they went through the process. The transition itself is a physical, mental, emotional and spiritual battle that must be faced and fought on all fronts. This will fully resolve the whole person into acceptance, whereas the journey toward wholeness and healing is only meant to resolve part of the person into acceptance within those aspects involving a broken

control. It takes direct loss to get each person's attention, threatens them at an individual level, and triggers every past issue within Self. Fear of abandonment is the primary issue. This experience communicates that one is about to lose everything they most value. Loss must become acutely painful and real before they begin to pray for and/or look for help. That which is easily attained is taken for granted, and often disrespected. Good things never come the easy way.

Bottom line. It's time to grow up, take Self Responsibility, become accountable before God, examine Self, and resolve past issues that contributed to the person one became before the crisis occurred. The point being, if no crisis came forth, no one would bother to take stock of their lives and examine what happened in their past that brought them to the place of believing their pain and suffering was caused by their midlife spouse. The unwanted emotional bomb was only a trigger for a journey that would have happened anyway. It was only a matter of time before one or both spouses would begin a journey that forced the other into their own journey.

Both journeys are solely about the individuals walking them, but something must trigger this inner examination. Most of the time, it's a major life's event, like a death or a spouse who has gone into emotional crisis. Each of these events are beyond the affected individual's control and provide the lesson that each individual controls Self only. Regardless of how many attempts one makes to manipulate and control what another person does, they fail. Failure is

---

relationship. It's up to each person to choose to examine their own half of what they brought into said relationship.

necessary, because each spouse must walk their own journey. No one except God can help.

The Journey to Wholeness and Healing

This journey of both spouses is called the Journey to Wholeness and Healing. It is important to take this personal journey for one's self, not for the midlife spouse. Through this journey, both spouses are to become emotionally mature from the same process. The journey is different for each spouse, but the result is the same, leading to a time of emotional peace and stability as one truly accepts and learns to love Self in ways not possible before.

As the left-behind spouse walks their own journey and applies the lessons learned, they help the growth of the midlife spouse. Change in one brings forth change in the other. But change in oneself must be faced honestly and sincerely, with the purpose of change, growth and becoming all God intended. Growth does not complete itself in just one aspect. Every trial is designed to grow in one of many directions. God is the guide in this journey, and if one is open to Him throughout, they will learn more than imagined.

The Way Forward

Every life involves a journey, and every journey has a purpose. The beginning of any journey, willing or unwilling, begins within the one who blazes their own trail. This journey begins within Self, because that is where every answer resides. There will be areas of life that need to be cut away and put to death. Every journey leads into more than one type of death. Every death leads into a new beginning, a new perspective, and a new journey that leads into greater things.

When the midlife spouse turned away, the left-behind spouse was put on a path not of their own making, but a path that now becomes all about them. This path is a journey one takes after suffering a major break in relationship. The journey toward wholeness and healing is triggered by a relational break and is emotional, involving one's relational choices.

This is the continuation of an emotional journey that should have been resolved in puberty, but because the aspect of emotional growth was missing, it was left unresolved. In this journey, one is called to resolve what was in them that chose their marriage partner. This issue has its roots in childhood and is based on how parents taught and modeled being in relationship. Until this is resolved, the individual will continue choosing partners who reflect the unresolved emotional issues contained within Self. In addition, one is called to own their contributions that led to the total break of the marriage, regardless of who made the decision to break it.

If one chooses to accept this journey and rise to the challenge, they will have nothing to lose and everything to gain!

<u>The Journey of Both Spouses are Attached</u>

The journey of the midlife spouse and left-behind spouse are attached and either spouse can cause the other to become stuck. Each spouse literally keeps the other spouse constantly engaged in their individual drama, cycling consistently until one does something to break the cycle.

The bulk of the responsibility for keeping both spouses moving forward falls to the left-behind spouse, the one not in crisis. Considering the left-behind spouse is charged with standing strong as the stanchion for the marriage, it is key for them to begin their journey and learn to emotionally separate from the midlife spouse.

It is also key for the left-behind spouse to begin learning the lessons of life as quickly as possible and continue their journey forward. This is regardless of whether the midlife spouse decides to grow or walk away. One is not responsible for the choices made by others, but is responsible for learning about Self, taking care of Self, and looking inward to target areas that need change, growth, and improvement.

If the left-behind spouse is not willing to focus on Self and their own growth, the midlife spouse will slip further and further away. Somewhere within their mind, the midlife spouse knows that change is needed, and they will look to their own spouse for that kind of leadership. When none is forthcoming, they can eventually turn away and the marriage will end for good.

Most mistakes are made when the left-behind spouse focuses too closely on their midlife spouse, trying to fix or control the process. One must learn to distance completely from the midlife spouse and release everything until the later time of accountability.

Another grave mistake comes when the left-behind spouse takes a victimized attitude of, "I didn't do anything wrong, therefore, I don't need to change." The midlife spouse needs to see their left-behind spouse standing for the marriage while also moving forward, taking the journey to wholeness and healing. When the midlife spouse sees a negative attitude, they can decide to shut the door that leads back to the life they once knew. That same door can be shut both ways and for different reasons on both parts. Ultimately the decision to stay or go belongs to both spouses.

Becoming the Opposite

Just as the midlife spouse becomes the opposite of what they were, the left-behind spouse becomes the opposite through the journey to maturity. One must become direct opposites of what they were before. God looks at personalities and, if one allows, He causes them to become the opposite of what they were before and uses them to bring about circumstances they wouldn't normally bring about due to their personalities. What one would normally do is not what they should do. One must do the opposite. Why?

To experience all facets of one's personality and face everything they are. In preparing for the second stage of life, all facets of personality must be brought forward and integrated. In this process, God works to bring about the new. It's as though He puts each person on the potter's wheel, which causes a breakdown of the old Self, bringing about the fashioning of the new Self. Through this trial, one is repeatedly thrown against the wheel until they come back together (are integrated) into someone totally new. In one's mind, they see what didn't work before and so, they are in the process of changing into someone they weren't before, just as their spouse has become the opposite of what they were before. The personality of the midlife spouse undergoes the same changes, and should reintegrate into a different person, if they allow the changes to come.

At times, change is resisted. This is where faith is exercised, and one must allow God to make the needed changes, while driving out fear. Becoming the opposite is a necessary part of growing up and moving forward, as one learns to handle any situation and the changes within must happen.

Questions to Consider in the Journey Forward

- Can I let go of those who have not achieved their own Self growth because I have determined that I will no longer be used, abused, misused, controlled, and manipulated?
- Am I willing to overcome those emotionally-based issues that were passed on to me as a wrong emotional legacy?
- Can I learn to become the emotionally mature adult God seeks me to attain, as my ongoing journey toward wholeness and healing continues forward?
- Am I willing to walk this hard journey of being remade, recreated, and rerouted so my past does not define my future?
- Can I commit to work through the difficult process of change, growth and becoming that will bring pain, knowing I have nothing to lose and everything to gain?

Chapter 15

If something is easily attained, there is no challenge. Without a challenge, there is no interest.
Without interest, there is no pursuit. Without pursuit there is no goal.
Without a goal, there is no fulfillment, and without fulfillment, life becomes empty.

The past marriage died a destructive and painful death and will never be resurrected or restored to its former state. Those who seek the old marriage will not find it. Change, though unwelcome, cannot be reversed. The only thing to do is move forward and learn to embrace the process of the midlife crisis. In time, it brings the left-behind spouse to a crossroad of choice, where they choose for better or for worse, then move forward into the resulting consequence.

It's been said that the left-behind spouse has the final say in choosing to continue or end the marriage. Every decision, every aspect, every trial runs a two-way street, with both people facing the same things, the same change, growth, and becoming while learning the same lessons. Every crossroad, though faced at different times, presents the same choices to both midlife spouse and the left-behind spouse. The left-behind spouse does not have the upper hand in making decisions during this emotional crisis. Every decision made is about the one who makes it, and no one person has the right to decide for another.

As stated earlier, these life journeys, though taken at different times, yield the exact same points of decision, crossroads, and life's lessons that all people are supposed to learn. Though the couple is married, their growth is from an individual stance. Everyone faces their own times of choosing their path. Each path chosen will either lead toward a time of reconciliation when the midlife crisis has past, or lead away from the midlife spouse, which leads into an unknown future. This unknown future will eventually reveal whether the decision made was for the best or is filled with regret. Why regret? Because one did not earn their way out of the marriage. Meaning, the left-behind spouse did not stay the course, walk their own journey, and utilize their time wisely for Self. In addition, coming into a fuller understanding that the only way out of the trial is through the learning of life's lessons.

These are learned and internalized in part by making a stand that will teach about finishing what one has started, honoring commitments and vows made rather than walking away from a situation one feels is too hard. God knows what is best for each person. He knows what each one can bear, and He will not put more on anyone than they can bear without asking Him for His help and strength to continue standing in the face of adversity.

The one who searches for help is the one seeking hope. No matter how the midlife spouse was before their crisis came and devastated their marriage, the left-behind spouse still loves them. Because of this existing love, the left-behind spouse can make the choice to Stand for their marriage. Whether they choose to Stand for a time or for the entire crisis is totally up to them.

Marriage and God | The Marital Covenant

When trouble begins, divorce becomes an easy option, a weakness, if you will. It's easier to run than to make a Stand for what one knows is right[1]. When people run from problems, they run into worse problems. There are consequences for abandoning a marriage in deep crisis, regardless of who caused said marriage to go down that road.

God has a divine purpose for everything He orchestrates, brings and binds together. As mentioned earlier, the past issues of each spouse complemented the other's issues, making both spouses a fit for one another. This union was never a mistake. God, who orchestrates marriages, never makes a mistake.

When the left-behind spouse learns to love unconditionally, they no longer base their outcome on what the midlife spouse does. The midlife spouse destroyed their half of the marriage when they shattered their vows. But they did not shatter the vows of the left-behind spouse, nor did they destroy the other half of the marriage. Each person is responsible for honoring their own promises, vows, and actions or for facing the consequences for not honoring their half of the marriage. The choice of the left-behind spouse is to Stand for the marriage or walk away.

---

[1] Not to mention what divorce does to children, and the real struggle that "blended" families go through, including the issues that are created in those children of divorce.

Because of the marital covenant God used to join the couple together, no matter what happens, He still sees them as One Flesh. What affects one will always affect the other, until God chooses to release one or the other at His discretion. The promise and vow made included staying together for better or for worse, for richer or for poorer, in sickness and in health, until death parted the couple. This word "death" means physical death. No other kind of death applies in this circumstance.

God's word says it is better not to vow than to vow and break the vow. This isn't just about the midlife spouse. It's also about the left-behind spouse. The soulmate connection between these two people will not break. It is God-created and God-strengthened. A person can run, but they cannot hide. Their problems and the torment associated with those same problems will follow them. New lives will not fix old problems because the only person one cannot run and hide from, besides God, is Self. And Self is where the problems originate.

It Takes Two | The Marital Covenant

A lifetime of living with someone within the state of marriage is the main emotional vehicle in which all life's lessons are to be learned. It takes two people to do some things that one person cannot accomplish on their own. That is, if both people in the marriage are willing to stand firmly through the storms of life that try to tear the couple apart.

While it's true the midlife spouse is responsible for their own work, the left-behind spouse becomes responsible, through their own work, in helping the midlife spouse once they return home. And they always return broken. If the midlife spouse didn't return in a broken state, the left-behind spouse would not learn how to help bear their load. It's a major part of the vow, for better or for worse. Of course, the left-behind spouse can choose not to accept the committed sin of the midlife spouse, but all things can be forgiven, overcome, and transcended by trusting God to help them learn[1].

Standing is not for the faint of heart nor for those who avoid their own journey in part or in full. The only choice one has in this trial is to choose to stand or walk. The rest is in the hands of God and the midlife spouse.

Called to Stand | The Marital Covenant

God, who created the marital state and knows the future, encourages people to make a Stand for their marriage early enough in the midlife crisis to prevent the left-behind spouse from walking away. People often get confused thinking to do what God wants, when the actual choice is theirs. Not every marriage will make it through, and the reasons for this are unique to each person walking this road. It is not so much that the marriage was not meant to come through,

---

[1] Galatians 6:1-10

but more about the people who make a choice for what they think they want.

Many are called to Stand, but few will obey God and stay the course. Why? Because it is human nature to want something without having to work for it. To have a reconciled and restored marriage will require obeying God in all things, doing the difficult inner work, and making the sacrifice to Stand in the battle for the restored marriage. It will require giving up control of the situation and letting go of what the midlife spouse does. And it will mean choosing to listen to one's intuition (the still small voice of God that does not shout) and choosing to follow those inner instructions into eventual resolution. People are tempted by the path of least resistance. Yet those who obey God in all things receive His promise of marital restoration at the end of a full-lived-through stand. For "The battle is the Lord's."[1]

To Stand requires faith in God and in the midlife crisis process. It also develops patience to withstand and perseverance to endure. As one stands in strength, one comes to look in hope for a time when the trial will end. One does find that, in time, their focus moves away from the marriage and centers upon Self. This is a good thing because it takes dropping the emotional rope to show the midlife spouse what they are losing. People often want what they can no longer have, and, once they discover the emotional door is closing, the midlife spouse often panics and begins moving toward the left-behind spouse. However, there are no guarantees, because the only sure thing is what the left-behind spouse chooses to do for Self. And

---

[1] I Samuel 17:47

remember, there is always a chance the marriage may not resolve as hoped because the midlife spouse may make choices the left-behind spouse cannot or will not accept.

To Stand or Not to Stand

Choosing to Stand or walk away is about the person making the choice. In this same choosing, there is no requirement to believe in anything. God is not going to make anyone do anything they do not choose to do. God gave all people free will. This allows them to choose according to their will with the understanding that for every action, there is a reaction and a consequence.

One would still be required to legally end the existing marriage before dating or going into another relationship. Otherwise, adultery would be committed on the part of the left-behind spouse as well. If one chooses not to Stand or chooses to stop their Stand, they will still need to take their journey to wholeness and healing in full. Why? Because people tend to choose partners based on their state of emotional growth. If a left-behind spouse chooses to end their marriage and not journey to wholeness and healing before starting another relationship, another emotional crisis will happen. It is only a matter of time.

The Determined Stanchion

Standing is deciding to wait without waiting, to move forward without moving on, and choosing to wait and see if the midlife spouse might decide to rebuild a relationship with the left-behind spouse. In Standing for marriage, one begins the process of becoming a true and determined Stanchion for what is right.

To be a Stanchion is to shine the light and become the draw for the lost. But it is not the spouse one is Standing for, it is Self. And with the passage of time, one realizes the Stand is to provide an opportunity for Self-growth, maturation, and faith. A Stanchion is called to lead the way forward, not just for the marriage, but for the path their heart knows is the right way. Without the strength of a Stanchion, one cannot even hope to Stand for marriage, for Self, or for their family.

In spite of everything, the determined Stanchion learns to move forward in the strength and confidence only God can provide, embracing what God has in store, even though the future is uncertain. Regardless of where the road may lead, the Stanchion keeps walking forward, as they experience a greater Self-awareness. They also come to realize their spouse in transition is on this same journey and the only difference is that each aspect learned occurs at differing times.

There is hope, there is always hope, as long as love remains. There's something to be said about honoring marital vows and staying with it, no matter what comes. For the determined Stanchion Standing for marital reconciliation, know that God's heart is toward the sorrowful, broken and devastated. He will help, strengthen, and heal the one who Stands.

Why Divorce does not have to end a Stand

God created male and female, and marriage was created for a lifetime. Jesus spoke of one door for walking out of a marriage – the door of physical adultery.[1] If one is experiencing physical abuse in their marriage, they should run away and not return. Unless one is threatened with physical harm, the marriage should not be ended, especially if there is still love in the heart for that spouse. God does not allow a person to be released from this covenant for emotional abuse. Emotionally abusive words can be dealt with through setting boundaries on bad behavior.

According to God's Word, the state of marriage is sacred. Marriage is defined as a Covenant created between God, one man, and one woman, meant to last through everything life offers. They bind themselves to each other and learn to love one another. A major midlife crisis should not make any difference, because this falls into the category of "for better, OR for worse." Divorce should not be an option, unless it becomes a matter of life or death.

Unfortunately, a midlife spouse will think to dispose of their marriage simply because Satan tempts them with the idea of "greener grass." This greener grass is not just a third person. It is also temptation that seeks to relieve an inner pain that is not easily understood. However, the choosing of a wrong path will lead into greater pain. Nevertheless, the midlife spouse only sees what they want to see at the time they experience emotional tunnel vision. They seek to cast off all responsibility in their bid for freedom. But regardless of which detour they choose, destruction awaits them. Filing for

---

[1] Matthew 16:18

divorce with barely a thought for the consequences is one of these of destructive maneuvers.

Why do some midlife spouses file for divorce? The midlife crisis is not caused by the marriage itself. However, the fact that the midlife spouse rebels against being legally bound to their spouse makes this crisis a marital problem. The midlife spouse, as explained in earlier chapters, suffers immense emotional pain. In spite of the different paths, they may attempt to avoid the facing of Self, there is one area they seek to blame for their ongoing pain: their long-standing marriage.

When the midlife spouse turns their attention to the marriage, they see it as one of the emotional traps of the past. At the time of the unwanted emotional bomb, they sent this relationship to its death (in their minds) and when they turned against their spouse, they emotionally destroyed the marriage. All that was left was the legal tie.

There are three questions the left-behind spouse will face when presented with the possibility of divorce:

- Is it possible to reason with or talk the midlife spouse out of filing for divorce?

    One could try to reason with them, but it could make the situation worse. Exercise caution if this route is taken. If the midlife spouse threatens divorce every time, they don't get what they want, a divorce may not be on the table. It's a manipulation tactic. If the subject comes up, simply state, "I do not want a divorce and I will not help you get one."

Most midlife spouses do not go further than threats because the work involved in filing for divorce puts the responsibility on them. They would rather have the left-behind spouse do all the work, so they can shift blame. If the left-behind spouse does not want a divorce, they should not be manipulated into filing.

- Can I slow the process of divorce?

Yes, one can slow it down, but consider each move carefully. The left-behind spouse knows the midlife spouse and what they are capable of doing. Some midlife spouses will fight in a vindictive way, with the intent of trying to take everything from the left-behind spouse. Others will give the left-behind spouse everything out of guilt. It is suggested the left-behind spouse make certain the marital assets are protected from the midlife spouse, if possible. If the midlife spouse is engaged in an affair, the money spent to finance the affair should be redirected back into the household. This is not a time of being concerned with making the midlife spouse angry. This is about making sure the left-behind spouse and any children at home are cared for. This is not vengeance, but consequences for wrong actions against the marriage.

- Can I stop the divorce from happening?

Depending upon the state or country one lives in, a divorce might be put aside or on temporary hold. But if the midlife spouse is determined, they will find a way to get what they want. The midlife spouse bears the entire blame for choosing this path into legal dissolution of their marriage.

One could try all three options and the divorce may still finalize. Even with the knowledge that wrong decisions are made that lead into wrong actions, sometimes the only choice is to let people do what they want. Most midlife spouses are stubborn and insist on making the biggest mistakes in their life. They will say they "have" to do it, or they are "driven" to it. Letting them fall may be the only way they will learn the most important lessons in life.

Make no mistake; there are consequences for every action. Good or bad is subject to the boomerang effect. If an action is good, it returns better, and if an action is bad, it returns worse. God is serious when He speaks of hating divorce, and when He speaks of people reaping what they have sown in corruption. In addition, He also understands that the innocent are not to blame for what a rebellious person chooses to do, because the divorce is not about the left-behind spouse. If the midlife spouse had not been married to his or her current spouse, this would have happened to someone else, so the midlife spouse's actions are not, in any way, a reflection upon the left-behind spouse.

It does not mean there is no hope after a divorce is filed and pushed through by the midlife spouse. People often think all hope is gone if the process of divorce is started and finished, but the hope that remains, (if hope remains), is not based on marital status. Hope is based on the love that remains within the heart. Hope is not based on the positive or negative actions of the midlife spouse. Hope is about the left-behind spouse who chooses to continue to Stand on the Marital Covenant from which God has not released the midlife spouse.

Midlife Spouse Remarriage to Affair Partner

When a midlife spouse commits adultery, they cause the death of their marriage. Death is a finality that cannot be reversed. Bear in mind, death can be physical, emotional, mental, spiritual and relational. The ending must be accepted as it stands and will never return to its former state, whether the midlife spouse divorced, divorced and remarried, or committed physical adultery. The old marriage is dead. Hope can still exist, but the ending of the current marriage must be accepted to move forward, whether for a later reconciliation or for the gift of healing and maturity.

When the midlife spouse remarries their mistake, the door directly back to the left-behind spouse closes for good. A different door can open for reconciliation with the left-behind spouse, but there is much more to overcome. Reconciliation, though possible, can take years. The more damage done, the more the left-behind spouse is called upon to overcome. Since God doesn't recognize the marriage of the midlife spouse with the affair partner, the midlife spouse would not be committing sin nor adultery in returning to the wife of his youth.[1]

---

[1] A typical midlife spouse can have multiple affairs, yet not file for divorce, and if there is still love within the heart of the standing left behind spouse, they can eventually be reconciled, even though there is much to overcome.

However, the left-behind spouse may not allow the midlife spouse to return because the adultery and subsequent remarriage are too much. This option for the left-behind spouse would be acceptable in the eyes of God. The act of adultery removed the left-behind spouse from further obligation and binding to the midlife spouse. Though the left-behind spouse is released from their obligation at the time of physical adultery, the adulterous midlife spouse remains bound and obligated to the left-behind spouse, no matter what they do. In the instance of a midlife spouse who is denied reconciliation, they go through the same wounds and emotions they put their left-behind spouse through in the beginning, as everything comes full circle.

The remarriage of the midlife spouse to the affair partner may be legal in the eyes of man, but it is illegal in the eyes of God. God does not recognize a remarriage based on adultery nor does He release the midlife spouse from the obligation of the left-behind spouse. In the remarriage, time is a significant factor in the relationship. Both partners have distorted perceptions, which shatter over time, as the illusions they think they have found in each other give way to a hard, cold reality. The midlife spouse will suffer extended and difficult consequences for this mistake because they have introduced the emotions of another into the union. They will suffer even more for what they must do toward the affair partner in order to return to the left-behind spouse. What goes around comes around. If one deals misery, misery will return to them worse than it was dealt.

God can also choose to deliver the left-behind spouse from their marriage. He can throw various roadblocks influencing the situation to make a return impossible. Remember, He knows the future and can choose to move in ways that will either encourage or prevent reconciliation.

The left-behind spouse will know if/when it is time to give up on marriage reconciliation. God will provide a clear sense of direction and release, but also allow the left-behind spouse to decide what they feel is best, knowing consequences for their decisions are on them. He does not hold the left-behind spouse accountable for the midlife spouse's actions toward the marriage. The fault belongs to the midlife spouse. If the midlife spouse marries the affair partner, the left-behind spouse is released. The Lord will not hold that against the left-behind spouse.

Whatever the left-behind spouse needed to learn from this journey to wholeness and healing must be learned before the left-behind spouse is released from the marriage vows. There are additional lessons to be learned, and God will lead the left-behind spouse into them.

Left-behind Spouse Remarriage to Another

Left-behind spouses who divorce and remarry are not as happy as they claim because they did not do the work to resolve Self, their issues, nor their marriage before getting into a relationship that distracted them from their journey. If one can walk away from a marriage knowing they did everything to save the marriage and still failed, that is better than reacting out of anger and entitlement, divorcing, and finding another relationship to fix the problem. The issues remain and will be faced again.

Chapter 16

Trying to absorb this information about your journey forward and the journey of
your midlife spouse will be overwhelming. Take this step by step. As more strength is gained,
find more answers to questions and put the pieces into place. Give Self the grace of time.

Just as there are eight stages (six stages and two healing processes) in the midlife crisis, the left-behind spouse also journeys through eight stages (seven stages of learning what is wrong, one stage of learning what is right) beginning with Full Emotional Devastation and leading to Wholeness and Healing. The journey of both spouses is identical, containing the same lessons. Starting, navigating, and finishing the journey takes time. Each person is different, their issues and the time it takes to resolve are different, but there are more similarities between the two spouses than one might realize.

The stages are listed below, with more detailed information following.

Eight Stages of Healing for the Left-behind Spouse

    Stage 1. Full Emotional Devastation
    Stage 2. Denial
    Stage 3. Bargaining
    Stage 4. Emotional Rock Bottom
    Stage 5. Deep Mourning

Stage 6. Crossroad of Choice
Stage 7. The Journey toward Wholeness and Healing
Stage 8. Acceptance, Forgiveness, Healing

Stage 1. Full Emotional Devastation

The day the midlife spouse said their feelings had changed, they gave the speech of, "I love you but am not in love with you", and discovery was made that the midlife spouse was not happy or was involved with someone else. Death of the relationship then occurred, triggered by the one who said they wanted out. The problem then lies within the left-behind spouse who chooses not to accept the ending of the relationship. Any loss is hard to accept and navigate through, because death doesn't just show in physical form. There is always a grieving period that requires an emotional, mental, and even spiritual journey to navigate.

The Emotional Bomb

The emotional bomb leaves the left-behind spouse feeling lost and afraid, betrayed and abandoned. When asked why, the midlife spouse cannot provide a clear explanation for this seemingly sudden emotional change, or they blamed the left-behind spouse for every bad feeling. It's hard not to take them seriously.

Their words were confused, disjointed, and their minds jumped from one subject to the next. They became distant and hateful; they flinched if touched by the left-behind spouse. Worst of all, they acted as if their spouse was the last person on earth they wanted to be associated with. None of this was true in the years preceding this direct dropping of the emotional bomb, things seemed fine.

But in all honesty, when the two first met, only their good sides were shown. Shortly after the marriage, the game of pursuit was over, and in their minds, there was no reason to treat their spouse that way anymore. Various negative shades of this selfish midlife spouse had been seen before, but their spouse either forgot them or rewrote history. Why? Because of fear that someone would say the marriage was a mistake. Hear this: The marriage was not a mistake, each person married someone they needed for their own growth, and vice versa.

There is no way to remedy the situation, strength cannot be found, devastation sets in, and the left-behind spouse can't eat, sleep or escape depression. Eventually, they reach out for help as things are not coming back together as hoped.

Their Script | Your Pain

The biggest mistake the left-behind spouse made was choosing to lose Self in someone they would never control. They trusted the midlife spouse to "keep you" and they didn't. So, the left-behind spouse is left to find their identity that was lost before the midlife crisis. Because of that, the left-behind spouse made the mistake of blaming Self for the problems that were in their midlife spouse.

Because of their projection, justification and angry confused spewing, they influenced the left-behind spouse into believing everything they said about their marital past. Their words were devastating, disastrous and destructive. The most damage is not what is face directly through the events we control, but what we are forced to face indirectly, through other people and events we cannot control.

If the midlife spouse spoke of wanting a divorce, or if the left-behind spouse discovered their relationship with another person, they think the marriage is over. Despite their devastation, after begging, pleading and crying, with no positive results, they feel it is best to end the marriage. However, they are unable to take this step and become rooted in fear and confusion as to how this happened. Emotions cycle that leads to feelings of sickness, alienation, betrayal and inability to function. All these combined aspects cause the left-behind spouse to ride an emotional rollercoaster that leaves them confused and disoriented.

To try and fix the situation, the left-behind spouse demands the midlife spouse to stop the nonsense. They attempt to rationalize the situation by suggesting maybe their midlife spouse has had a temporary breakdown, need help or counseling, and end with a plea.

As the various skirmishes continue, the left-behind spouse pulls out every emotionally charged weapon in their vast arsenal. Inciting guilt and shame to appeal to their sense of fair play and doing everything they can to change this unacceptable state of mind. All to no avail. In a last-ditch effort, the left-behind spouse brings up the children and the midlife spouse turns away. The angrier and more miserable the left-behind spouse is, the more justified the midlife spouse feels.

If they choose to speak at any great length, accusations pick up verbal and emotional speed. Their unknown and unrehearsed script goes like this:

- "You don't understand me."
- "You don't meet my needs."
- "I am no longer attracted to you."
- "My feelings have changed and will never go back."
- "I swear I am done with you."
- "This isn't about the children; they won't be harmed."
- "If you were not reacting this way, I wouldn't have to distance myself from you."

According to their self-imposed justification, the left-behind spouse is at fault for everything. Their further unknown and unrehearsed script goes like this:

- "If you had not done xyz, I would not have done xyz."
- "If I can't get away from you, I will xyz."
- "I never loved you, never should have married you."
- "Nothing within the marriage was ever good."
- "I am not willing to give you the chance to fix what you did that caused me to be this way toward you."

The left-behind spouse has not changed but the perception of the midlife spouse has been altered by them. They made choices that caused them to leave the marriage emotionally and mentally, and they divorced the left-behind spouse in their mind and emotions. Therefore, the left-behind spouse is no longer of use to them. Why?

Because what they did and the choices they made were not about their left-behind spouse. Their spouse no longer fits their emotional needs, therefore is expendable to them. (This is a lie, but this is their perception.)

Within the context of the midlife crisis, there is a death of emotional feeling by the midlife spouse, who buries their affections for the left-behind spouse under layers of justification. (They do this to justify their wrong actions.) The death of the marriage soon follows as the midlife spouse emotionally destroys the bond that once held them to their spouse. They leave their spouse behind, so they can figure out who they are apart from them. It's what midlife spouses are driven to do; it's not what they want to do, it's what they feel they must do.

Alternatively, if there is another person involved, the midlife spouse states in a seemingly calm and clear-headed way, the other person understands them, knows them, will be so much better for them than you are or would ever be. Some midlife spouses even go as far as describing how this other person is really their true soul mate and describe how they feel so much better, more alive when they are with them. This sends the left-behind spouse into deeper shock, causing them to stop listening, and walk out of the room because they can't stand to hear anymore.

Finally, the left-behind spouse understands there is no arguing with someone whose state of mind seems to be in one set place. Within a short period, the emotional divorce becomes complete, and the marriage is within the grip of an emotional crisis. The previous life has ended, and nothing will ever be the same.

Steps for Moving Forward

- Protect resources and finances. Formulate a plan and stick with it. Set a firm boundary in the financial area.
- Schedule a physical. The midlife crisis takes its toll on the left-behind spouse. If necessary, get antidepressants to calm and clear the mind, so the journey within Self can begin.
- Find a group with understanding of the midlife crisis.
- Put an end to destructive behaviors. You are not going to get what you want. When your spouse went into the tunnel, your marriage and your life as you knew it died. All the crying, begging, pleading, clinging, and/or demanding will not fix anything. Those behaviors will only cause more damage, as disrespect from the midlife spouse will only increase. Pushing, pressuring, anger and asking questions of the midlife spouse will only serve to drive them away because those things are considered controlling and manipulating.

Stage 2. Denial

In the beginning, there is only emotional pain that brings a time of self-victimization, issues of abandonment, and a fear of what the future may hold. The left-behind spouse tries to live in a self-imposed protective bubble of deep denial. This stage causes serious problems, because one cannot move backward, they can only choose to stand still (which allows them to temporarily exist with some semblance of sanity), or move forward, which will eventually move them along into the bargaining stage. To have to bargain means they must accept something is wrong.

There are five stages of grief: denial, anger, bargaining, depression and acceptance. In an ideal end to the grieving process, one is called to accept closure and navigate into a new beginning. Unfortunately, there are people who stay in denial that death of a relationship has occurred. But life goes on despite all that happens. Regardless of the kind of death faced, a process involving full resolution of past life must be completed so one can move forward. It's up to the individual to seek closure to this kind of death which involves an emotional, mental, and often spiritual journey. All stages of grief must be worked through versus refusing to move forward.

The passage of time brings forth more change, as one discovers there are positives in learning to accept the death of a life once known. Once change is embraced, an emotional door opens into a new life; but it's up to the left-behind spouse to choose to accept the closing of one door in favor of opening a new door.

Full emotional devastation, and denial are still present even as they move into the next stage of Bargaining.

<u>Stage 3. Bargaining</u>

"Can't you just come back?", "If you will stop all of this nonsense, I will do whatever you want."

This stage can become lengthy, filled with self-pity, tantrums, and bargaining. The behavior of the left-behind spouse suggests they carry out a reverse form of emotional blackmail, aimed at Self. In addition, they are willing to sacrifice self-respect to do whatever is suggested by the emotional terrorist, the midlife spouse, to reverse the situation. But none of these behaviors work. The midlife spouse will take everything offered that will benefit them and continue taking until nothing is left. They will do what they want, regardless of what the left-behind spouse says, does, thinks or tries to negotiate.

Emotional devastation, denial, and bargaining combine, which sends the left-behind spouse into a deeper emotional spiral. Well-meaning people pressure the left-behind to spouse to get a divorce, to stop living in denial, to get over their devastation and move on. Yet, the left-behind spouse cannot "move on," and they question, "Whose life is this, anyway? Not your decision, mine!"

If the left-behind spouse seeks help, there is an ongoing struggle with, "Your spouse is in a midlife crisis, which has put you on a road not of your own making, but makes the journey all about you, just as their crisis is all about them."

Caught betwixt and between, this unrelenting pressure moves the left-behind spouse to a crossroad of decision as they understand there is no going back. They can approach this crossroad with a decision to Stand for the marriage or file for divorce. Either way will be painful, and the struggle between choosing continues until rock bottom is hit.

Stage 4. Emotional Rock Bottom

The pain of the left-behind spouse has intensified to the point one cannot take anymore. The bottom of deepest pain has been reached, and the only way to look is up. There are two realizations;

- The journey is at a crossroad of choice.
- It all takes time to figure out.

These realizations trigger the next stage of misery in this continuing journey. It hurts to know everything has been lost, and grieving that loss is quite normal.

At this point of the journey, acceptance becomes a major part of each stage. For every aspect faced, one must accept the current stage before one can move into the next.

<u>Stage 5. In Deep Mourning</u>

This is the first time the left-behind spouse understands their marriage and past life are dead and gone. This is a time of deep and heartfelt grieving for what could have been. This is also where the next realization comes that they have no control over anyone except Self, their actions, reactions, and responses. This brings forth the next stage where a choice must be made.

<u>Stage 6. Crossroad of Choice</u>

At this point the emotional cycling intensifies as pain increases. This is not what the left-behind spouse signed up for, and confusion grows despite the reality seen. It is not unusual to reverse into emotional cycling for a time to prevent Self from committing to a choice. The left-behind spouse knows what should be done, but because of continued emotional cycling in stages one, two and three, they struggle with knowing the right thing to do for Self.

Meanwhile, the crisis becomes worse, spinning further beyond the left-behind spouse's control. A path of least resistance tempts them, saying that leaving the marriage and getting into another relationship will fix them. Of course, common sense dictates that new partners will not fix old problems.

In the long term, the left-behind spouse faces two choices:

- Continue cycling in a negative emotional rut. This is not solely an external journey, because external changes will only cause an internal problem to worsen. Besides, negative and materially based external changes do not feed inner growth, nor do they lead to lasting peace. People are often guilty of avoiding their internal chaos by using other things, people and circumstances to distract them from the necessary inner work.
- Turn inward to understand what issues triggered when the midlife spouse made decisions that did not take them into consideration and were made against their own sense of right and wrong.

Eventually, a choice is made, and the left-behind spouse moves forward onto their chosen path. The most desirable choice, and the hardest emotional road, is the one that leads to wholeness and healing. It takes time to understand why one must look within Self for necessary change rather than looking at the mistakes and choices of the midlife spouse. But once this aspect is overcome, the journey to growth, change and becoming begins. Those who choose this harder emotional road continue to walk through these stages.

Those who choose the easier emotional road temporarily leave this journey to wholeness and healing. It is only a matter of time until they cycle back.

Stage 7. Begin Journey toward Wholeness and Healing

The journey to wholeness and healing is taken in parts and three realities are seen. The reality of past Self, past spouse, and past marital dynamics. Emotions are triggered within these realities, and steps are taken toward healing. This journey encompasses replacing emotionally immature beliefs and behaviors with mature ways of thinking and being. It also moves the left-behind spouse into change, growth and becoming all God intended.

Growth is painful because change requires a reworking of old beliefs and behaviors. In time, the left-behind spouse will become what God means them to be in Him. Emotional maturity requires change that brings growth. This puts each person in a state of becoming greater than they were instead of remaining less than they can be.

Emotions Triggered Within these Stages

- Anger/Rage: With the crashing of one's world, the intense emotional fire, fueled by intense anger, burns hot because the left-behind spouse is not only angry at the midlife spouse, but also at Self. They intuitively know they must get control of this emotion. In time, as the anger and rage run their course, they bring forth three things:

- Clarity: Clarity of the situation as it stands, which causes the rose-colored glasses to fall and shatter on the emotional floor.
- Death: The former love will die a sudden death, with a new love to be reborn a short time later as God's human gift of Unconditional love. The death of all things always leads to a new beginning.
- Peace: As the rage breaks, it leads to peace, which is the next aspect necessary for a time of healing. Peace comes before the final three stages of Acceptance, Forgiveness and Healing are navigated.

<u>Reality of Past Self</u>

This reality begins with exercising Self-focus and looking into the Self-reflective mirror that reveals their identity. The basic question asked: *"When all of the layers and past identities are stripped away, who am I?"*

While the midlife spouse runs from this question, the left-behind spouse faces Self in honesty. One can expect to see shades of the person they once were, along with all areas that need change, growth and becoming, including past childhood issues that must be confronted for the very first time.[1] This is the most difficult step, as it involves digging deep within Self to recognize emotional damage and repeating patterns.

Once the damage is seen, the next stage is finding the root of the damage, then accepting and resolving the damage. This deep work

---

[1] It would be rare for someone to not need this leg of the journey.

brings about recognition, acceptance, resolution, forgiveness and healing, which all take time. This aspect of Self-examination can be frightening, especially to one who has never done this before.

It takes a journey into the past to resolve the past, which creates a better future. But pain from the past can become an obstacle. Many times, people need to give permission to Self to delve into the painful emotional memories because one must feel these past emotions that contributed to who they are. Then they must face the past issue that created the feelings, resolve them into forgiveness, and receive healing.

Since not everyone is knowledgeable in the way of Self-examination, there are two ways to do this.

- God is always available to answer questions through the gift of intuition (the still small voice within that does not shout), if this aspect is contained within oneself.
- If this aspect has not yet been developed, one may choose a trusted individual to listen and help while the gift of intuition is developed.

If one learns to stay in tune with God, they will always know what to do and when.

Change, Growth and Becoming

The most important part of this journey is discovering and remaining true to Self. When one walks the first part of this personal journey, they learn to see Self in full reality. In that process, they learn to exercise clear honesty within Self, releasing avoidant thinking, which comes through the lies once told Self. One learns to accept they are flawed and broken within. They find issues that need targeting, examination, and healing. They learn to see areas within Self that need improvement. Upon seeing these areas, they begin work that leads into change, growth and becoming what God means them to be.

Change is about learning to find Self-worth, Self-esteem, and Self-confidence within rather than looking for validation in other people. It involves taking ownership of unresolved issues, failures, inadequacies and lack of Self-love. If personal pain exists, healing has not completed.

Each person's inner journey is tailored to fit their individual Self. People must find their own way through this journey, which is designed to be a positive benefit for the left-behind spouse. However, the changes made need to be permanent and for Self rather than as temporary changes made to control or manipulate the midlife spouse.

Steps Toward Healing

- Realize that nothing the midlife spouse has said or done is even close to being about you. They made their choices.

- Realize you do not have control over anyone except yourself, your actions, your responses and reactions.
- Dig into Self to learn what it was in you that attracted such a weak and commitment phobic person to begin with.

Reality of Past Spouse

As the left-behind spouse heals the issues within Self, they see the past issues within their midlife spouse. They see what it was within Self that attracted their midlife spouse. The left-behind spouse will understand that there are issues in both spouses that have nothing to do with the midlife crisis. There was something wrong long before, or they would not have given one another a second look. This enables the left-behind spouse to make various changes in the way they relate to their midlife spouse, including setting boundaries against certain behaviors.

The marriage to the midlife spouse had its foundation within a set of unresolved past issues that attracted the left-behind spouse to them. There is a certain emotional "familiarity" in the midlife spouse that completed a deep need within the left-behind spouse.

To further explain, humans are creatures of habit, especially in the emotional arena. People subconsciously search for, attract, and often marry someone who is most like an emotional pattern they recognize, with which they are familiar. Emotional patterns are defined as behaviors, ways, and actions, which were learned in childhood. Since most childhoods were dysfunctional, their past family dynamics developed an emotional pattern that needs to be outgrown. They cannot complete this growth process alone, so they subconsciously need this new person to help them learn.

Therefore, the attraction seems familiar and brings a certain comfort, as if they are emotionally returning home. In short, familiarity is an attraction. Relationships were created for learning to grow and become what one was intended to be. But change must consistently occur within one or the other for this process to happen.

In any relationship, things stay the same until one of the partners change. Changes made within the left-behind spouse will be recognized by the midlife spouse and will affect change in them. Because change is hard for most people to embrace, it will take time for the change in the left-behind spouse to trigger change in the midlife spouse. Given time, the midlife spouse will challenge the change, but the left-behind spouse should hold their ground firmly, standing on boundaries set. There will be people unwilling or unable to accept changes and walk away.

<u>Steps Toward Healing</u>

- Learn to see your midlife spouse for who they are, not for what you thought they should have been.

<u>Reality of past Marital Dynamics</u>

The past marriage comes under scrutiny and is seen in its reality. There was a dysfunctional way of interacting because both partners brought baggage into the marriage in the form of emotional issues that fed off one another. After the left-behind spouse is seen past and present, only then will the left-behind spouse see what was wrong within the marital dynamics. This is a major part of continuing toward the change, growth and becoming aspect within the ongoing journey.

The entire marital relationship must be dissected and examined to determine each person's part in the breakdown. That's not to say the actual decision to destroy the relationship lies upon the one who was betrayed, but each one has a part to examine. Why? Because each one played a part in the events that led up to the time of the actual destruction of the marriage.

All steps must be navigated in order, no steps can be skipped. It takes Step one (Reality of Self) to bring about Step two (Reality of Spouse), and then, as steps One and Two are combined, step Three (Reality of Past Marital Dynamics) is seen more clearly. The left-behind spouse will see the past relational mistakes made, and with new knowledge, will see how each situation, on both sides, should have been resolved.

To have a new marriage in the future requires change within both people, but the honest effort of one person is necessary to create and start the process of positive change to hopefully assist and/or trigger change in the other. The road toward changing another will only come about when one chooses to begin positive change within Self. Someone must begin this process of change, growth and becoming.

Steps Toward Healing

- Determine the wrongs within the past marital dynamics so they are not recreated.
- Set proper boundaries and limits on certain behaviors of the midlife spouse to trigger change within them. Hold firmly to those boundaries.
- In keeping with set boundaries, make it clear that until they figure out what sent them down the path of adultery, there is no hope for the marriage to renew, reconcile and rebuild.
- Choose to stay the course regardless of where it leads, with the understanding the midlife spouse will continue to be who they are while you remain true to Self.

The Crossroad of Decision

Seeing the reality and truth of Self, Spouse and past Marital Dynamics is often hard to process. However, what is known cannot be unknown. As this reality comes into view, it exposes a harsh truth that leads to a loss of feelings. The already frayed and torn feelings of love die a sudden death and hope dwindles[1]. This adds insult to injury and prompts new consideration for an old question, decided on earlier in the process but cycling back for reconsideration. What is the question?

---

[1] These feelings are normal and will pass in time, as one resolves the crossroad and begins to walk forward.

Am I Still Willing to Stand for this Marriage?

Standing for the marriage becomes a choice, not a necessity, as the reality of both people and the relational past comes into view from the vantage point of a broken and destroyed marriage. The midlife spouse is seen for who they were and who they are. Remaining to be seen is what they will become in the future.

Though an emotional door is open in cases of physical adultery, God hates divorce and if He can positively influence the left-behind spouse to choose the harder emotional road, He will assist the left-behind spouse in the process of overcoming the sin committed against them.

When the midlife crisis is finished, God will assist in renewal, reconciliation and rebuilding a marriage that has been fully ravaged by the emotional storm of the midlife crisis. Until then, there is a long emotional road to be walked by both people. One learns to take one day at a time, step by step, and trust God to assist the midlife spouse in overcoming their personal battles[1].

Feelings will not carry the left-behind spouse through this uncertain time, so hope and love become a solid choice. One needs to draw on God and on the prior commitment "for better or for worse."

---

[1] The left behind spouse cannot give direct help, but there is nothing stopping them from giving such help as listening, validating, encouraging, loving, caring, compassion and praying for the pain-filled midlife spouse.

Moving into the Second Half of the Journey

Once all three realities (Self, Spouse, Marital Dynamics) are faced in full, they will overlap, combine, and trigger the second half of the journey. In turn, this leads into an intense learning to accept, forgive, and heal. The second half takes longer because the first half involves learning what is wrong, and the second half involves learning what is right.

Encouragement

People often struggle with God for allowing bad things to happen, and for setting certain requirements for change, growth and becoming. They become angry with Him for seemingly turning His back on them as they try to stand up after the emotional bomb. When nothing they do works to return a situation to its previous state, they choose to turn away from God, which is the worst thing to do. It is hard to understand, but there are benefits that come from this mid-life trial.

When we learn God is the only one who has control over all things, we see that all things will work to the good of those who love the Lord and are called according to His purpose.[1] Holding on to hope makes life easier to bear. A hopeful attitude makes a difference.

Acceptance. Forgiveness. Healing. Time.

---

[1] Romans 8:28

Stage 8. Acceptance, Forgiveness and Healing

Much change, growth and becoming occur during the first half of the journey, revealing what needs to be accepted, forgiven and healed within Self. The second and longest portion of the journey includes these three aspects that bind the first and second half together to create a whole and healed person. Those three aspects are Acceptance, Forgiveness and Healing.

Acceptance

There are several aspects of acceptance that involve recognizing, then accepting oneself and one's spouse as being fallible, therefore capable of making mistakes. There are also the past dynamics of the marriage, recognizing that neither person within the union was perfect. It is not easy to come to terms with the past, but the past is set in stone and living in the past makes the future elusive. It would sound as if forgiveness would be a fit for that last sentence. In one sense, it is, but within the realm of acceptance, it is not. One cannot forgive unless one chooses to accept. After a while, the left-behind spouse learns to accept Self, their midlife spouse, and the past marital dynamics, in that order.

Forgiveness

The next phase of the journey involves forgiveness of Self, the midlife spouse, and one another for the contributions made that led to the breakdown of the past marriage.

One of the hardest things for the left-behind spouse to work through is the midlife affair. The affair is the most common temptation for the midlife spouse to fall into because it is the hardest sin to work through, overcome and forgive. It is also the sin that causes the left-behind spouse to think they were at fault or caused it to happen. They personalize, rationalize and justify the choice of the midlife spouse to fall into adultery, which is wrong. The left-behind spouse cannot help the situation. One can only learn to accept it, learn the lessons associated with it, discern it for what it is, and separate Self from the sinner's sin, set boundaries on it, and hold onto love for the midlife spouse.

Forgiveness is a process within a process, completed in layers[1]. It is for the benefit of the left-behind spouse, not the midlife spouse. Within forgiveness, the person who committed a sin against another stands last in line, until all other layers are peeled off.

There are many layers to work through, but as they are slowly peeled away, the person who committed the wrong is exposed. Peeling away may look something like this:
- Why the deed was done
- When it was done
- Triggers resulting from the why and the when
- The damage done

---

[1] God forgives the sinner all at once, but He knows everything and there is nothing He is required to work through. Although He forgives us for sin when we ask Him, our consequences are not held back, and they shouldn't be. If one does a wrong, one must face the consequences and learn the lesson. Consequences brought forth through His orchestration of the circumstances are simply saying the same thing, "You reap what you sow."

- The negative feelings caused
- One's personal feelings
- The additional fallout
- Any additional questions needing answers
- The final questions that may not get answered
- Direct consequences chosen to dish out because of what was done

If the midlife spouse sinned against the left-behind spouse and is granted forgiveness, the midlife spouse does not have the right to ask the left-behind spouse to withhold personal consequences for the sin committed. Neither does the midlife spouse have the right to refuse to help the left-behind spouse heal from the damage done.

Healing

The aspect of healing arrives when all aspects of the previous journey are resolved. Healing does not come at once, but it does come as one moves forward. This is where God does His most wondrous work. Some healing occurs at certain points of the journey, as the person going through will accept and forgive some things en route. However, at the very end, God aids in such a thorough healing that all emotional aspects become a fact instead of a feeling. In many cases, some, if not all, memories are removed or allowed to fade over time.

Time itself is the greatest of all healers, helps change perception and perspective, and allows a person to integrate a past event into the fabric of their lives. People change, grow, and become throughout life, but this experience is the main key for confidently moving into a more productive future.

This will not happen all at one time. However, regardless of whether the marriage is reconciled, these things should still be accomplished within, as these lead into full emotional maturation, which is the goal of the midlife transition period.

Emotional Triggers

An emotional trigger can be described as ripping open a past wound and are a symptom of post-traumatic stress disorder. Until these wounds are healed, they will continue to be ripped open repeatedly. A good example is the emotion experienced by the left-behind spouse due to the affair of the midlife spouse. Even after the midlife spouse returns home, feelings are not automatically healed. There is a process one goes through that leads to healing. One must accept that the event happened, fully forgive, and only then will healing come. It is the same process regardless of the emotional event experienced. These triggers came into existence at the time of the wound, whether from a personal past, the issues caused by the midlife spouse, or issues compounded by the midlife spouse's actions during their crisis.

There are three factors that help in the healing process: Time, God and the willingness to go through the process that leads to full emotional healing.

The Healing Process

There is an emotional understanding we must have to heal within. We learn to relinquish power we do not have over what other people do, and we learn to detach from the actions of others we think are intended to hurt us[1].

To heal, one must face Self squarely, examine each trigger and the issue within that brings forth the trigger, determine where the root of the trigger originated, and resolve each issue. To reach full emotional healing, one must walk through the road of pain and emotional triggers. It is the only way to complete the process in full. A lot of inner Self-sorting must be done to get at the actual source of the emotional memories.

Steps to Process and Heal from Emotional Triggers

- Look at the actual event that happened and process it.
- Learn to accept what happened, understanding what was done and that it was not about you. (It was about the person that did it against you.)
- Give permission to Self to revisit the emotions that were repressed or not grieved during that event. Dig out each feeling, lay it on the table, recognize and feel it, then work through it.
- Grieve whatever loss is brought forth.

---

[1] These actions hurt the one doing these things, but at times our emotional understanding has not reached that level of growth.

- If one refuses to accept and embrace what happened, the triggers continue. Why? Fear that it might happen again, fear that one will never be happy, fear that things will never resolve. Fear is at the root of refusing to accept and forgive. If one cannot accept and forgive, they cannot heal and will cycle continuously.
- Emotional healing of triggers is a process that takes time to complete; it does not happen overnight.

Once a full emotional healing takes place, the emotional past becomes a fact that is remembered rather than a feeling to be relived. Forgetting is a by-product of full emotional healing. The only aspects not forgotten are the lessons learned from the experience.[1] Once this process has been worked through and resolved, future traumatic events are less likely to cause aftershocks leading to emotional triggering. This is because inner issues have been resolved and one has learned to sort the emotions, so memories will not trigger going forward.

<u>Detachment</u>

Before detachment, the emotions of the left-behind spouse are often raw, painful and sensitive. Deep emotional pain, because of what the midlife spouse is doing, demands one to either detach or entertain other thoughts to escape the pain. The faster one detaches, the better they will be because everything the midlife spouse does will affect them in a positive or negative way.

---
[1] There is no purpose in pain unless you learn lessons set before you.

Total detachment, also known as emotional distancing, is a necessary tool of emotional survival. It is a complete and conscious removal of the emotional overtones of the stress brought on by the crisis and the actions of the midlife spouse. Detachment is for one's own emotional protection, as the left-behind spouse learns to view the situation through a lens that does not involve the emotions.

Detachment assists in the emotional healing of the left-behind spouse, so their emotional strength can rebuild. Without the emotional strength necessary, the left-behind spouse is unable to navigate the full journey to wholeness and healing.

In detachment, one's feelings are placed in an emotional box and set aside until a time when these can be dealt with, controlled from a point of strength, and without feeling the negative effects of emotional devastation. When the left-behind spouse sees and interacts with the midlife spouse from this place of detachment, they see a stranger with a problem, but are not be inclined to fix it.

As detachment takes a deeper hold, the emotional rope is eventually released as the emotional distance widens between the spouses. Detachment must occur, and some healing of raw emotions must happen before the three final stages of acceptance, forgiveness, and healing can be navigated.

Growth requires that each person must own their past mistakes and their contribution to the total breakdown and death of their marriage. Rage must be fully resolved into clarity to experience death of the former love and receive peace in what has happened. The resolution of these things make acceptance of what has happened easier, so forgiveness and healing can come forth.

One cannot accept anything if one cannot detach. One cannot forgive if one cannot accept. One cannot heal if one cannot forgive. Each aspect is a process within a process, and each process requires completion of one before the next begins. Each process goes in step, detaching to see how everything lies, without coloring it with negative emotion, and then accepting what has happened, forgiving the deed, and healing.

<u>Why and How to Detach</u>

Detachment will be the hardest thing to do. It will be a process and may take years to completely detach because fear gets in the way. The main fear is that one will lose love for the person they are detaching from. This will not happen. One will know love still exists within; however, they will be unable to access it for the time they are in total detachment. If accessed, it would draw the left-behind spouse back into the drama of their midlife spouse, and the love hidden within would be destroyed by their wrong actions. Staying in total detachment protects the love hidden within.

The process of "uncoupling"[1] must happen and is a major part of growth in learning who one truly is, where they end and everyone else begins.

---

[1] Uncoupling is part of what happens during the total separation of Self and spouse. It involves learning to cut all physical, mental and emotional connections. It is a total disconnect the left behind spouse must reach before they finally decide to work on Self. The midlife spouse has already uncoupled from the marriage and this is for the left behind spouse to do the same. It is a learned behavior that accepts the right of the midlife

Why Detach?

- It is a protection of and within Self to guard against emotional self-destruction and nervous breakdown.
- It protects Self from the influx of feelings one cannot handle.
- It disconnects from the drama of the midlife spouse and allows one to step aside so God can work within the situation.
- It enables one to observe the midlife crisis from an emotional distance of love that remains. There is still an element of love for the midlife spouse that is hidden and preserved for a later time.
- It releases the midlife spouse to their own journey.
- It enables the left-behind spouse to their own journey, to put focus on Self, examine oneself and do the necessary work of change, growth and becoming.
- With detachment, the left-behind spouse can move forward (but not move on).
- It enforces a form of "no contact" where the emotions are removed so one can heal within Self.
- It puts one on the outside looking in from an emotional standpoint, so one can understand more about separating the behavior from the person.

---

spouse to affect a total disconnect. One can't make someone stay with them if they don't want to, so the left behind spouse must go through a process of uncoupling from said marriage.

Detachment ensures the left-behind spouse is protected from further emotional hurt. It becomes necessary during the journey to wholeness and healing to view one's life as it had been and to see the past reality of the midlife spouse, so these aspects can be seen without experiencing an emotional breakdown. In that process one begins to accept, forgive and continue to heal in a more complete way, from the damage that occurred because of the midlife spouse. God works in circumstances such as these. When the time is right, feelings for the midlife spouse will return as one begins building a new connection with them later in the crisis.

Communication in Detachment

This is a time of learning emotional survival. Communication with the midlife spouse will require patience and be a mental challenge. The left-behind spouse has the possibility of coming through the marriage by following their intuition and allowing God to lead.

Detach from the situation as quickly as possible and lessen contact. The more one says, the angrier the midlife spouse becomes. Below are four methods of contact that may need to be enforced during the crisis, at various times.

No Contact

For many people, contact with the midlife spouse is difficult because they are so broken. They have enough trouble functioning without taking continual abuse from the midlife spouse.

If the midlife spouse walks out, use "No Contact". This will give the left-behind spouse time to gather emotional strength, regain perspective, and have space to heal. Learn to care for Self. Stop pushing, pressuring and pursuing someone whose heart and mind are turned away.

No contact can last as long as one needs. The mindset of the midlife spouse is to keep track of, control and manipulate the left-behind spouse. They are arrogant and think everybody wants them. Most of them are involved in affairs. Contacting them will bring rejection and/or frustrate any expectations the left-behind spouse may have.

Within No Contact, emergencies dealing with children, family situations, etc. are allowed. Remember, the midlife spouse is notorious for playing tricks and faking emergencies, so the left-behind spouse needs to hold firm to the No Contact boundary. If it can wait, do not respond. Do not be hateful toward the midlife spouse while going No Contact, but take a calm, firm stance. When the left-behind spouse heals enough to handle what the midlife spouse is doing, break No Contact and attempt to deal with them again.

No contact depends on the situation at hand and is strictly for the left-behind spouse and not used to punish the midlife spouse. There is no rule about going No Contact. This can be done as often as needed to get space for Self and give the midlife spouse space to work on themselves. The waters can be tested at any time by the left-behind spouse to see how a situation stands, as long as this can be done without expectations.

No Initiating Contact

"No Initiating Contact" is used in the case of the midlife spouse who has vanished or has told the left-behind spouse they don't want contact. The left-behind spouse is advised to let go and allow God to do His work. Let the midlife spouse initiate contact.

Go Dim

If the midlife spouse is still in the home, the left-behind spouse is advised to "Go Dim" in communication. Speak as little as possible. Answer questions briefly, kindly and politely. The less said, the less the midlife spouse has to use against the left-behind spouse for justification or angry spewing.

Go Dark

"Go Dark" means no contact of any kind, regardless of what happens. This aspect is used, for example, when a midlife spouse has pushed for and attained divorce, yet still tries to have it all. This is not punishment. To Go Dark often forces the midlife spouse to face the consequences for their actions and shows they have lost the left-behind spouse due to their actions to end the marriage legally. Sometimes this is enough to turn the midlife spouse around.

Emotional Repackaging | Living Authentically

At the end of any emotional crisis comes a time of repackaging one's Self. To reconstruct Self on the inside, a deconstruction must first take place on the outside. This requires an emotionally based trail that requires a process of being broken down before being built up. One aspect of this change involves choosing the many emotional pieces that lie within Self, locking those pieces together like the pieces of an emotional puzzle, and choosing an acceptable way we present Self to others.

This is not a mask. It is an honest presentation that begins within and involves how others see us. It is part of learning to live in an authentic way without selfishness, lack of consideration for others, lack of love and without becoming totally consumed in Self.

Living authentically is not necessarily about what one does but is based on an honest knowing of Self. This reflects in speech, behaviors, and how one relates to others. There is no waffling, negativity or defense involved. One lives unapologetically, without pride, arrogance or negativity, knowing where they end and someone else begins. Living authentically involves setting boundaries that let people know what will and will not be tolerated in the way of emotional behaviors, which shows a clear definition of what they are about without compromising their core Self and values.

This aspect of emotional repackaging of Self may return many times in a lifetime. Our perception, perspective and emotional growth dictate that a self-examination is necessary from time to time, as we do change based on our place and time of emotional growth.

Reclaim Personal Identity

Both marital partners lost individual identities within each other during the years of marriage, raising children, etc. Both took God's concept of "one flesh" several steps too far, developing a co-dependent relationship instead of an interdependent one. Both forgot how to think for Self. Even in those rare times when one did think for Self, they were pressured into the way of their spouse.

Now both partners are on the same journey – to reclaim individual identities. Hopefully both will grow and become who God meant them to be. However, this involves a journey of major proportions and a quest that leads deep within Self to achieve this reclaiming of the person originally intended. Then, each partner will learn to go further into the deeper aspects of outgrowing the immature emotional qualities that are connected with their own past issues.

From there, each person learns to set firm but loving behavioral boundaries, learns to love and accept Self, and becomes more peaceful within. While this growth is occurring, the left-behind spouse learns to detach completely, because anger only clouds one's thinking and this same anger will drive the midlife spouse away.

In this season of healing, the left-behind spouse will find their true Self[1] and take the time to become reacquainted, thus reclaiming their personal identity.

Reclaiming Emotional Power

The key to mature change begins with the reacquisition of personal emotional power. This will positively influence the gradual evolution of the dynamics within a given relationship. Additionally, this involves one who is willing to walk the ongoing journey toward wholeness and healing for Self. In this process, one learns the lessons of life, learning more about who they are, what they stand for, what is right and wrong behavior, and learns to stand on their own, strong and sure. It all takes time, but time is never wasted when used for change, growth and becoming.

As a result, this yields one who is willing to make a solid stand against manipulating and controlling behavior. If the left-behind spouse does not throw down the gauntlet of change and become strong enough to directly challenge wrong behavior as they come to know it, the situation will either cycle repeatedly or become worse.

Reclaiming and Defending Self-Respect

There are some normal aspects one can put into action to reclaim Self-respect. One way is by letting the midlife spouse have what they say they want, communicating that if they are in relationship

---

[1] The true Self is the person their midlife spouse once fell in love with.

with the affair partner, they cannot be in relationship with the left-behind spouse.

It is not uncommon for the midlife spouse to ask the left-behind spouse to agree to something they know is a sin according to the Word of God. The midlife spouse wants to get away with anything and everything, even to the most immoral of sin. They test boundaries and limits of propriety on the part of the left-behind spouse, who is advised to stand firmly against their actions in a position of strength, truth and honesty, and in clear defense of Self-respect. The midlife spouse must learn what is and is not acceptable to the left-behind spouse, and the test that is brought forth the most is the one that pushes against the morals and scruples of a person's character.

Sin will take a person farther than they ever wanted to go and cost them more than they ever wanted to pay. As the left-behind spouse, know the difference between right and wrong, do not cave, and do not do anything that destroys the core character of Self. Nothing is worth lowering standards to that of a sinning and rebellious midlife spouse. Many times, doing the right thing will involve defending Self-respect. Do not back down in weakness nor allow wrong behaviors to be acted out against Self. Do not support immoral behavior of the midlife spouse because they will use that support as manipulation to pull the left-behind spouse in deeper.

The left-behind spouse sets the standard and lays the boundary to defend Self-respect. Nothing is worth sacrificing Self-respect to try and save a marriage. That marriage ended when the unwanted emotional bomb was dropped. The responsibility for maintaining solid moral ground falls on Self.

Godly Intuition

There are clear spiritual dimensions to every trial. During the midlife crisis, various spiritual gifts are triggered into existence because of the immense amounts of stress endured. One of those gifts is our Godly intuition. Some people refer to this gift as their "gut instinct" and "listening to the gut." Intuition is a still small voice that never shouts. God can and does speak to His people.

To be clear, the voice of the Lord and the gift of intuition are the same; there is no difference in this aspect. Our intuition is the still small voice within. It is there for a purpose, because God is determined that He will not leave us alone to face these things. In addition, there will not always be someone around to help or intervene.

One of the most effective ways to develop intuition is to accept everything heard, regardless of whether it is good or bad. It is very informational. If one remains open, their intuition can tell them what is ahead. Learn to trust that still, small voice and recognize that God is working, even as He speaks to the heart. As one remains open, their spirituality will increase through the trial. This is positive growth.

Intuition reveals itself in different ways and within different people. To allow God to speak within the heart, our free will must be submitted to His will. One can choose to accept pieces of information that come from nowhere at times. These pieces are designed to help us "know" certain things, without having to understand how they are known. Godly intuition is peaceful; human intuition is fearful.

Using this intuition requires a mental and emotional adjustment as well. As it becomes a normal part of life, one no longer fears what comes. The more intuition is used, the stronger it becomes. As one submits to and trusts their intuition, they gain confidence in Self to help others, which helps improve their own situation.

Intuition is also useful in strengthening trust in the Lord, to know it is Him who speaks and to hear each time He speaks. Because God always seeks to directly connect with His children, it is wise to develop the gift of intuition. Take time to seek Him for every need. In time, this much needed gift of intuition and discernment will be developed and come into alignment.

Final Emotional Processing

After change, growth and becoming are complete, a final and full emotional processing is finished, which enables the left-behind spouse to accept the events of the past, forgiving the midlife spouse and Self. This is true whether the left-behind spouse decides to stay in their marriage or embark on a new relationship in the future.

This is a long journey that will eventually resolve in a positive way. The left-behind spouse who walks this journey to completion will show a positive attitude and the entire journey will be perceived as an opportunity that led to positive change, growth and becoming. They will find new purpose, as their emotional feet walk a completely new road that leads to learning about the aspects of the prior journey taken. They will know that no matter what happens, they will be just fine, and will be able to face the future knowing that God is in control of all things.

This part of life's journey does not have an actual ending but goes to a new beginning as life goes on, change continues, growth deepens, and becoming what God means for a person to be takes on new meaning. Everything learned and internalized will provide a person with the Emotional Tools of a Lifetime, meant to be consistently drawn upon.

The result of the left-behind spouse's growth is a permanent inner peace. This same journey, which began with a negative life-changing event, should end on a positive note as the whole and healed person progresses forward into the future.

If one does not take and complete this journey, they will repeat the same mistakes with a new person. If there are unresolved issues within, one will always attract someone who complements the remaining issues, and the cycle will return from another aspect. Complete the journey in full, the first time around. Put nothing on hold and setting nothing aside.

Chapter 17

It's their mistake, they will have to live with it.
It's their problem, they will have to solve it.
It's their process, they will have to work it out for themselves.
The focus is now on you – your change, growth and becoming.

Dear Left-behind Spouse,

As a recap of the midlife crisis, here are the generalized points which should help and encourage you to move forward into your own journey of growth and maturity.

- You did not break them; therefore, you can't fix them.
- Their midlife crisis is about them, not you. This is their crisis, their problem. Do not make it your crisis or your problem.
- Everything they say, do, and decide is about them and not anyone else.
- The midlife spouse is a hurting person, so they hurt others.
- The midlife spouse does not need your help because they are responsible for choosing to either help Self or remain stuck in their crisis.
- You can try to influence the midlife spouse, but you cannot control or manipulate them into doing what you want. You control only yourself, your actions and reactions.
- The midlife spouse must emotionally regress and rewind back to the place their emotional growth was stunted,

stopped and unfinished. They will then progress forward to go through a necessary redevelopment process intended to mature them into the emotionally mature adults they were always meant to be.

- Early childhood damage created emotional issues that were stored away in the Shadow of the Psyche for later development. The child damaged early in life did not have the necessary emotional maturation nor the necessary emotional tools and knowledge needed to face, resolve and heal the damage at the time it occurred.
- Until the midlife spouse learns to look inside for the answers that have always been there, they will continue the emotional, mental and spiritual battle occurring on the inside of Self.
- The most drastic mistakes they will ever make come from the attempt to utilize outside solutions to fix inside problems.
- The midlife transition can be navigated in full without falling into sin. However, few transcend the crisis without trying to run from the emotional pain and turmoil that exists within.
- Most midlife spouses will destroy past connections they held and attempt to destroy everyone who stands in the way of their own Self-gratification.
- The goal of a whole and healed emotionally mature adult is a life of peace that knows happiness can only be found within Self. To arrive into full healing, the only way out is through.

- There is no situation God cannot deal with, work with, isn't familiar with, and cannot guide one through! As He teaches us to go forward, we learn the only way out is through, without shortcuts, without avoidance, and without using human aspects to try and cure something God does not mean to be cured.

For the one who learns and practices life's lessons, they will be given the opportunity to use, practice, and refine these lessons in helping others grow. If/when the midlife spouse returns home, the left-behind spouse will use these lessons to help them mature into the person God originally intended. But bear in mind, this will be a hard road.

Throughout the book, the life's lessons needed in the journey to wholeness and healing have been mentioned. Several of the more important life's lessons are included in this chapter to give greater detail, which include:

- Boundaries
- Change
- Control
- Letting Go
- Unconditional love

Boundaries

Boundaries are lines drawn between what is yours and what belongs to someone else. It is a clarifying line so there is no misunderstanding where emotional/physical distance is added to drive the point home. A relationship without clearly drawn boundaries is a train wreck waiting to happen.

The first sign someone has crossed a private line is an anger that rises within because one feels violated in some way. This is a warning to take heed because a boundary has been crossed or someone is in the process of trying to cross it. Set a firm boundary and be prepared to enforce it, and if necessary, with a consequence. If a consequence is set and not enforced, the boundary setter loses respect.

In crisis, the midlife spouse will push every limit set, every boundary laid, and unless the left-behind spouse puts an end to bad behavior, they will continue said behavior. To stop the bad behavior, the left-behind spouse sets a hard limit in certain areas of conduct. It takes a willingness to take an honest look within oneself and courage to target areas that need improvement, then making permanent changes that lead to growth.

The midlife spouse has no respect for anyone, including Self. The left-behind spouse learns to love Self enough to set boundaries, draw the line, and make it clear they are protecting Self from further damage. Boundaries are for the boundary-setter, not the person they are being set on or against. When a boundary is set, the other person has the choice to honor the boundary or walk away. Be prepared for either outcome. The midlife spouse may rebel, become angry, posture, etc., because they don't like the limit set, but once they realize the left-behind spouse will not back down, they face a decision. Accept the limit and show respect for the left-behind spouse or increase their rebellion in an effort to "punish" the left-behind spouse and influence them to back down from the set limit. Rebellion against the setting of boundaries is controlling, but the setting of boundaries is not controlling – it is exercising Self-protection.

One cannot worry about whether the setting of boundaries will drive the midlife spouse further away or draw them back. The midlife spouse is the only one who can decide what they will do, and when they will do it.

Summarized in the following pages are boundaries that can be set against the midlife spouse to protect Self and help them in their emotional journey.

<u>Boundaries Covered in this Chapter</u>
- Behavioral and Relational
- Behavioral Cycling
- Children of their Issues
- Communication
- Disrespect
- Guard Your Heart
- Midlife Affair
- Revolving Door
- Separation of "Me and Thee"
- Self-Care
-

Boundaries: Behavioral and Relational

There are many kinds and types of boundaries, such as time management, weight loss management, money management, etc. Through exercising these kinds of personal boundaries, priorities are set and straightened out.

There are also relational and behavioral boundaries. We teach people how to treat us, and if we allow people to treat us badly, they will do just that. Boundaries protect us and help us teach and re-teach people how to treat us. Through enforcing boundaries, people learn there are limits to what will be tolerated in the way of behavior.

If verbally abused, every person has the right to put a boundary on that behavior with a consequence of leaving the room if it continues. The fact the left-behind spouse finds it easy to quickly forgive and love denotes a lack of boundaries, both personal and relational. One should be loving and forgiving, but not to the point of allowing others to take advantage of or walk over them. No one can control what others do, but everyone can put limits on their exposure to the sin of others.

Sometimes one must enforce the electric fence of their boundary. Sometimes more than once. This will literally be shocking to any person who has been enabled in the past and will force them to pay attention to the new changes made and being enforced. That's why a situation gets worse before it gets better, at least for the one setting the boundary. People have the option to walk away from making an emotionally healthier choice, but the boundary setter stands firm on their own healthier choice to set the boundary, which is for Self.

Boundaries: Behavioral Cycling

A behavioral cycle starts when the same behavior crops up, is repeated, and there is no end to it. In other words, it circles without end. People do what we allow them to get away with, so the person who has triggered, or is repeating this cycle, must have help to break free.

When a clear cycle of unwanted behavior begins, either a confrontation must ensue, or someone's behavior must change, and that someone is the left-behind spouse. The behavior the left-behind spouse stands against determines the changes that must be made. This is solution-based thinking, which depends on what one is facing as to what must be done. If one thing doesn't work, another should be tried. Each person is different and may require a combination of things to bring about a desired result. No one can decide that for the left-behind spouse, who always has a choice and knows the midlife spouse better than anyone else.

There are situations when behavioral cycles continue into infinity because the left-behind spouse lacks the strength to make a standout of fear of losing the midlife spouse, who is already lost to the midlife crisis.

When boundaries are set, the left-behind spouse is growing, changing, and exercising the life lessons learned to change their own behavior, which will impact the behavior of the midlife spouse and stop the cycling.

Boundaries: Children of their Issues

As discussed in earlier chapters, the "children of their issues" are the basis for the midlife spouse acting out in total rebellion. Behaviors such as cursing, name calling, angry spewing, and attempted physical abuse. These bad behaviors literally cry out for behavioral boundaries. The midlife affair is the only exception to the rule, and an in-depth discussion of the midlife affair and setting boundaries are covered later in this section.

The midlife spouse will become angry when a boundary is set because no person wants to be told what to do nor held accountable within this respect. Yet, like children, there is a subconscious crying out for an emotional fence set against bad behavior. Until they realize the left-behind spouse is not backing down, they are subject to throwing tantrums and escalating their behavior, often trying the patience of the boundary setter. When they realize the left-behind spouse is not backing down, they are faced with two choices: honor the boundaries and limits set or walk away.

Even though the child within does all it does, and the left-behind spouse begins changing, the core personality will surface and test the left-behind spouse. Boundaries are still called for to break bad habits. Once the left-behind spouse knows what needs to happen to impact change, true change within the left-behind spouse becomes the task of breaking bad habits and bringing forth new ones within the midlife spouse.

Boundaries: Disrespect

The left-behind spouse should guard against allowing the midlife spouse to manipulating them into accepting disrespectful behavior, such as name calling, blaming, shaming or guilting. An adult simply sets boundaries and walks away, removing Self from the abuser's presence. This is the boundary for any negative comment that shows disrespect.

All personal and relational boundaries should become clear, defined and non-negotiable. The left-behind spouse deserves and should command respect and shoulder their own burden of hurt. Do not enable bad behavior, do not feed drama. Learn to heal Self, and pay attention to godly intuition that says back off, don't answer, leave it alone, etc.

Further, the left-behind spouse is advised not to approach the midlife spouse for attention and to resist allowing emotional insecurities to manipulate them into pursuing the midlife spouse. Allow space for the midlife spouse to approach; they dishonored the marriage, they cheated, so the consequences for their adultery is on them. Choose not to pursue them for anything. In fact, back off and wait them out. If they are being pursued, why should they give one thought to what they have done against their marriage?

Boundaries: Guard Your Heart

Every affair is about the cheating spouse, not the betrayed spouse. The only thing to be concerned about is the maturity and growth taking place within the midlife spouse. Details about the affair and the affair partner do not matter. What matters is that the betrayed spouse knows an affair happened, knows the midlife spouse is facing what was in them that sent them down this destructive road, and sees change, growth and becoming are in process, which ensures an affair does not happen again.

Knowing any detail is devastating, painful, and sometimes when too much is divulged, it can cause divorce. Why? Because the betrayed spouse's heart can't take the hurt. Discussing the affair keeps the emotional memory alive in both people, and healing cannot take place. In order to heal, one must feel the pain, but the first step toward healing one's past wounds involves a choice to let go of expectations that the betrayer will do all the work of healing both partners. The betrayed spouse must learn to face their own pain and heal their own Self.

Boundaries: Midlife Affair

Regarding the midlife affair, all the left-behind spouse can do is let the midlife spouse know that as long as they are in relationship with someone else, the marriage is over, and if they persist in walking this road, they will lose everything.

The following two boundaries need to be set against an adulterous spouse:

- The left-behind spouse will not accept any blame or responsibility for the affair.
- The left-behind spouse will not accept another affair, ever.

The left-behind spouse should be prepared to enforce both boundaries, especially the second one, with the appropriate consequences. One cannot make the betrayer love them or care about them, but one can learn to love and care enough about Self to defend Self-respect in this area. Something precious was taken with the previous affair that will never be returned and the left-behind spouse has every right to make it clear what they will and will not accept from that person in the way of future behaviors.

After making it clear that another affair will not be tolerated, the left-behind spouse is advised to back off and continue their own path to change, growth and becoming, letting go of expectations. It is not the job of the left-behind spouse to enforce, coerce and harass the midlife spouse into doing anything. One can make it clear the midlife spouse has a choice, but what they choose to do in the future will either help the marriage rebuild or cause the marriage to break down completely. But the midlife spouse must be left alone to choose to engage in their own work to heal Self and the marriage they destroyed of their own free will.

Boundaries: Revolving Door

There will be midlife spouses who are so rebellious, no matter what the left-behind spouse does, they use their home as a revolving door. However, the midlife spouse was only doing what the left-behind spouse allowed them to do out of fear of losing someone already lost to the crisis. In this case, the left-behind spouse must overcome fear and set firm boundaries to effectively deal with this continued disrespectful behavior that only adds stress.

Boundaries: Separation of "Me and Thee"

The most difficult aspect of this journey is convincing the left-behind spouse to take care of Self, learn who they are and what they want and need, and learn enough about Self to know where they end, and other people begin. This is the separation between "me and thee" that is part of the emotional, mental and physical survival. People simply do not want to learn to put the focus on Self to look within for answers.

The biggest mistake each left-behind spouse makes, especially in the beginning and not long after the unwanted emotional bomb drop, is to put their entire focus on the midlife spouse, in favor of neglecting their own journey.

The left-behind spouse needs to address their own hurt and not allow it to fester within. They are to stop, examine their feelings, separate what is theirs from what belongs to the midlife spouse, and realize the midlife spouse's actions, words, and ways are not because of anyone else. The midlife spouse makes choices based on their own selfish wants and desires.

The left-behind spouse wants to know how to fix, control, and manipulate the behavior of their midlife spouse. They disregard, disrespect and do not accept the decisions the midlife spouse made, and they are uncomfortable by the change they did not get to fix, control and/or manipulate.

The greater the emotional immaturity in the left-behind spouse, the more difficult to convince them that honesty is the best policy. One cannot control or manipulate their midlife spouse; but they can do everything for one's Self, even as one chooses to detach, distance, and relationally walk away from the midlife spouse. Cut all connections except for the Marital Covenant Binding that is God's to deal with, and one He won't cut.

It's the only way the left-behind spouse can save Self. To do otherwise would mean emotionally drowning in the vast problems of the midlife spouse. But the midlife spouse will drag the left-behind spouse down with them, because they are desperate to ensure they have someone to bear the blame, shame, and guilt for the decisions they have made. They do this by projecting these emotions onto the left-behind spouse.

Boundaries: Self-Care

Learning Self-care is not an easy task, but it is necessary to protect oneself from people who do not want to grow up and take responsibility for themselves. Self-care comes before Other-care. If one is not healthy, one can pass an unhealthy outlook to others. Everything we are and will be begins with Self, and Self-care helps us extend care to others. Not to take care of them, but to care for them.

One must learn to be content in Self and also learn that happiness, Self-validation, Self-esteem, etc., come from within. No one can make another complete. Acceptance of Self is important as we must live with Self for the remainder of life and know deep within what we can and cannot tolerate. We must trust Self to do the right thing, understanding that no matter what happens, we will be all right. Finally, one needs to give Self the emotional permission to feel as one chooses, without guilt, shame and thinking that changing Self will hurt others.

Every person has needs that will be met by others, but no single person can meet all those needs. One learns to prioritize the most important needs while learning to invest in Self and learning contentment with what one is given by their spouse. No one person can meet all the needs of another because each person has their own idea of what is important. This is where mature compromise is negotiated.

Life's Lesson: Change

Dear Left-behind Spouse, After the total rejection from your midlife spouse, you have an opportunity to become all you were created to be. Embrace this opportunity. Below are a few hard suggestions to work through to begin your journey into wholes and healing.

- The changes you go through are for you, not your midlife spouse. These changes are for you, so the same issues are not taken into the restored marriage or a new relationship. Everything your midlife spouse goes through will be the same thing you walk through. You will be tested in the same ways and learn the same lessons, day by day, for a long time. Both journeys are similar.
- All changes you make during this journey must be permanent. The longer you exercise these changes, the more permanent they become. As you change, you will see a difference in Self, in others, and in your midlife spouse. These changes affect everyone you deal with and open your

eyes to see things in others that were veiled before.
- Give this journey time to work itself out. Be patient. You cannot fix your midlife spouse. Your interruption in their journey will only frustrate them and prolong the process of their complete healing.
- Even after your midlife spouse exits the tunnel, there will be changes to come and a settling down that must occur. These things take time, patience, longsuffering, unconditional love, compassion, understanding, and a willingness to hang in there to see them through.
- No one in midlife crisis is the same, but the steps to come through are the same.
- Your marriage may survive; it may not. Do not let that worry keep you from growing and learning. Do not waste time worrying about your midlife spouse. They will come forward when they are ready, or they will not. You have no control over their journey. Do not get drawn into their drama. Learn to stand on your own.
- Understand that everything the midlife spouse does and says damages them as well.
- Understand that to ignore or attempt to avoid this journey will only bring it full circle, for you and your midlife spouse.
- Remember, God is with you every step of the way. Learn to call on Him, depend on Him, and listen to your Godly intuition for guidance.

Life's Lesson: Control

Life's Lessons involve the lesson of control. This lesson helps one learn the following:

- The only person one can control is Self, not anyone else. Change must begin within before a situation changes without. That means all control one thinks they have must be released, whether physical, spiritual, etc. This is the first and most important of Life's Lessons, simple yet hard to put into action.
- Practice emotional control; stay calm in conflict.
- Separate Self from others, knowing where one ends, and another begins.
- Understand how to separate the behavior from the person.
- Everything one says and does carries consequences, whether good or bad.
- One's character is an asset that should be guarded. It's a treasure no one can take away unless one allows that to happen.
- Do not partake in or enable the sin of another.
- Do not bear the sin of another on the altar of Self-sacrifice.

This bears repeating. The only person one controls is Self. For every action there is a reaction. For every action there is a consequence. Since one cannot control anyone except Self, that means change must begin within Self. If one chooses not to change, one cannot even hope for someone else to change.

Life's Lesson: Letting Go

Dear Left-behind Spouse,

You must let go no matter how painful it is. It is through the giving of this freedom that you may regain your midlife spouse. In letting go, peace will be attained; it is the peace you can have within the storm. Until that point is reached, there will always be confusion. It is through the clearing of the mind that the answers come from within.

The steps of letting go and letting God work are as follows:

- Let go and get on with your life as if the midlife spouse is not in it. To hold on, cling, manipulate, or try to fix them will only make matters worse. Gather your strength for the road is long and rocky. Find yourself.
- Recognizing unhealthy attachment.
- Release the desire to have "other" control.
- Work through the process of detachment.
- Reaching the final point of surrendering everything to God.
- Drop the emotional rope in full knowledge that no matter what you do, no matter what you say, no matter how many times you may seek to move and "block" someone's freedom to choose, they, like you, will always have a choice.

This is stepping back, and giving them what they say they want, with the realization that they might decide they don't want it after all.

In letting go, God is asking us to obey and surrender to His will. If we obey and fight to stay within His will, He can work within the heart of our midlife spouse. When we "let go" of the outcome, we align our relationship with God in the proper order. God first, us second, others third. The relationship with our midlife spouse cannot come between our relationship with God; otherwise, that makes the marriage or the midlife spouse an idol. Letting go of the midlife spouse allows God to work in their heart and life in ways you never could. God can do the inner work within the heart of the midlife spouse to help influence their decisions. He does spiritual work, true, but more emotional work because this midlife journey is about emotional maturity.

Life's Lesson: Unconditional Love for God, Self and Others

Dear Left-behind Spouse,

I want to close this chapter with a word of encouragement for the journey to wholeness and healing. God's unconditional love is available to you, and He will see you through this journey. You can lean on Him and depend on Him to carry you through.

To develop an interdependent relationship with God, one must first become solely dependent on Him. That is how a relationship with God begins. Now is the time to transfer co-dependency traits from humans to God. Our co-dependent trials and immature ways represent our burdens that we are encouraged to lay upon His shoulders, so He can deal with them. This represents our first attempt to let go of circumstances. These same traits and ways are related to our ongoing trial. As we let go of these things and give them to God, He enables and strengthens us.

As we grow, God slowly weans us from our former co-dependent ways that we brought to Him at the very beginning of our spiritual growth. This weaning is so slight it almost escapes our notice. It is necessary for us to learn to move forward in confidence, without fear, as He makes us overcomers within our circumstances. He teaches us to have confidence, faith, belief and dependence on Him, but also helps create a true and correct emotional, mental and spiritual mature balance within us.

He teaches us through life's circumstances of our everyday life. He walks us through the deepest valleys, assists us in scaling the highest mountain. At the top of each mountain, He reveals to us, in hindsight, what we need to know, learn, and as a result, add to our arsenal of spiritual, mental and emotional tools.

He is there to meet our deepest needs, to teach us what we need to know, to show us what His love looks like, to comfort us when we are upset, to be patient with us as we struggle to understand many things, and He is there as our best friend. He takes on our co-dependent tendencies, if we let Him, and He transforms us into the person we need to be in Him. Do not be afraid to lay these burdens on Him. He will walk us right through the process that leads from immaturity into a greater maturity. In His time.

Love for Self must exist before we can give and receive love from another. Two people in a relationship must learn this of themselves before moving on to greater intimacy. God asks us to begin our own growth maturity process to remove the garbage of our past that prevents us from loving Self as He loves us.

Love is a choice and accepts people at every stage of growth, every point of struggle. Love seeks to help but in a way that never allows a person to take the easy way out of accountability. Love sets boundaries because love must sometimes be tough. You choose to love although you may have to employ detachment to protect yourself from becoming hurt by angry and immature outbursts and reactions.

This same commitment to love is a point in reminding you not of what you are standing for, but for whom you are standing – first God, then yourself, then your midlife spouse. Remember, we love God because He first loved us. It would stand to reason He would love us simply because He created us as His own, to look like Him. We become loved because we chose to mindfully love without expectation, without being hurt, and without allowing someone who isn't showing us love to hurt us. That is how you can still love while remaining completely detached from the midlife spouse's actions, ways and continued rebellion.

I really wish I could reach out and hug all of you so hard, but this will have to do:

(((((((((HUGS)))))))))

I also wish nobody had to go through this crisis, and if I could, I would take your pain. However, as I know from personal experience, *the only way out is through*. And, just as I once did, you can do this, I know you can. I have faith in you. May God go with you, be with you, bless you, and guide you forward daily.

((((HUGS))))
Hearts Blessing